MARK COLVIN'S KIDNEY

By **Tommy Murphy**

Currency Press, Sydney

CURRENT THEATRE SERIES

First published in 2017
by Currency Press Pty Ltd,
PO Box 2287, Strawberry Hills, NSW, 2012, Australia
enquiries@currency.com.au
www.currency.com.au

in association with Belvoir, Sydney

Copyright: *Mark Colvin's Kidney* © Tommy Murphy, 2017.

COPYING FOR EDUCATIONAL PURPOSES

The Australian *Copyright Act 1968* (Act) allows a maximum of one chapter or 10% of this book, whichever is the greater, to be copied by any educational institution for its educational purposes provided that that educational institution (or the body that administers it) has given a remuneration notice to Copyright Agency Limited (CAL) under the Act.

For details of the CAL licence for educational institutions contact CAL, 11/66 Goulburn Street, Sydney, NSW, 2000; tel: within Australia 1800 066 844 toll free; outside Australia 61 2 9394 7600; fax: 61 2 9394 7601; email: info@copyright.com.au

COPYING FOR OTHER PURPOSES

Except as permitted under the Act, for example a fair dealing for the purposes of study, research, criticism or review, no part of this book may be reproduced, stored in a retrieval system, or transmitted in any form or by any means without prior written permission. All enquiries should be made to the publisher at the address above.

Any performance or public reading of *Mark Colvin's Kidney* is forbidden unless a licence has been received from the author or the author's agent. The purchase of this book in no way gives the purchaser the right to perform the play in public, whether by means of a staged production or a reading. All applications for public performance should be addressed to Cameron's Management, Locked Bag 848, Surry Hills NSW 2010, Australia; ph: 61 2 9319 7199; email: info@cameronsmanagement.com.au

Cataloguing-in-publication data for this title is available from the National Library of Australia website: www.nla.gov.au

Typeset by Dean Nottle for Currency Press.

Cover design by Alphabet Studio.
Cover image show Sarah Peirse. Photo by Daniel Boud.

Contents

MARK COLVIN'S KIDNEY

    Act One   1

    Act Two   44

Theatre Program at the end of the playtext

Currency Press acknowledges the Traditional Owners of the Country on which we live and work. We pay our respects to all Aboriginal and Torres Strait Islander Elders, past and present.

Mark Colvin's Kidney was first produced by Belvoir at the Belvoir St Theatre, Sydney, on 25 February 2017, with the following cast:

BRUCE FIELD / SENIOR PHYSICIAN / DAVID / PRIEST / IRANIAN OFFICER	Peter Carroll
WILLIAM COLVIN / JUNIOR PHYSICIAN / MARTIN / BBC RADIO JOURNALIST / TOM / CHARON / KANE	Kit Esuruoso
MARK COLVIN	John Howard
MARY-ELLEN FIELD	Sarah Peirse
PROFESSOR ZOLTAN ENDRE / JOHN COLVIN / CARL / LUCAS / BBC RADIO STUDIO GUEST / EMAD	Christopher Stollery
ELLE MACPHERSON / MICHELE COLVIN / CASSANDRA / BBC RADIO JOURNALIST / NURSE SUNITA / FRENCH PARISHIONER / AMERICAN OPERATOR / WAITRESS	Helen Thomson

Director, David Berthold
Set Designer, Michael Hankin
Costume Designer, Julie Lynch
Lighting Designer, Damien Cooper
Composer and Sound Designer, Nate Edmondson
Projection Design, Vexran Productions
Videographer, Xanon Murphy
Movement Director, Scott Witt
Stage Manager, Luke McGettigan
Assistant Stage Manager, Keiren Smith

The following is based upon actual events.

The play makes use of surtitles to display the source of quoted material, the translation of lines spoken in foreign languages and occasional scene settings.

The authors of the quoted correspondence have approved its use in this script. Messages, emails, transcripts and tweets are unabridged unless stated otherwise. Please note that the BBC Archives have not retained the broadcast of the 'Today' program on 9 August 2006, depicted in Act One Scene Four.

CHARACTERS

MARY-ELLEN FIELD, 63, an Australian businesswoman in the UK
PROFESSOR ZOLTAN ENDRE
ELLE MACPHERSON, 41, the supermodel
CARL, a US security guard
MARTIN, a US therapist
DAVID, a sex addict
BRUCE, Mary-Ellen's husband
CASSANDRA, a Tory MP
TOM, a young Tory staffer
MARK COLVIN, an Australian journalist originally from the UK
SUNITA, a renal nurse
EMAD, an Iranian man
CHARON, a Hutu refugee in Goma (near Rwanda)
LUCAS, a London lawyer
FRENCH PRIEST
MICHELE, Mark's wife
JOHN COLVIN, Mark's father
WILLIAM COLVIN, Mark's son
WAITRESS, who morphs into an anaesthetist
SENIOR PHYSICIAN
JUNIOR PHYSICIAN
BBC RADIO JOURNALISTS
KANE, ABC cadet journalist
FRENCH PARISHONER, SECURITY GUARD, CLUB MEMBER, LONDON TUBE ANNOUNCER, IRANIAN OFFICERS, DINERS

SETTING

Sydney, London and briefly Goma, Saint-Félix, Tehran and Washington.

/ indicates a point of interruption in a line of dialogue.

This play went to press before the end of rehearsals and may differ from the play as performed.

ACT ONE

SURTITLE: *'The following is based on a true story'*

SCENE ONE: NEPHROLOGY

SURTITLE: *'Prince of Wales Hospital, Sydney, 2012'*

MARY-ELLEN FIELD *is a brightly dressed, blonde 63-year-old.* PROFESSOR ZOLTAN ENDRE *is a small man with a large moustache, spectacles and a colourful bow tie. His desk is untidy with papers and files.* ZOLTAN *is flanked by two male colleagues—a* SENIOR PHYSICIAN *and a* JUNIOR PHYSICIAN.

ZOLTAN: So I might as well start by asking … Are you mad?

    They laugh. MARY-ELLEN *does not.*

This is the organ with the highest blood flow and workload. It releases hormones that help you produce blood and control blood pressure—all sorts of tasks this spectacular organ does—so by and large if it didn't filter the hundred and eighty litres a day and reabsorb most of that, then you'd disappear down the bog before lunchtime.

MARY-ELLEN: I know you have a statutory obligation under Australian law to dissuade me.

ZOLTAN: Not quite. Would anybody like a Coke Zero?

JUNIOR PHYSICIAN: No, I'm right, Zol'.

ZOLTAN: I have some in my bar fridge.

SENIOR PHYSICIAN: Not for me.

ZOLTAN: Mary-Ellen?

MARY-ELLEN: No I won't, thank you, Professor.

    ZOLTAN *gets himself a Coke Zero.*

ZOLTAN: Mary-Ellen, we'll be checking your family history, your cardiac and renal status, all transmissible diseases, infections that might be resident. Cancer is transmissible, polyps in your colon, for example.

MARY-ELLEN: None of which I have. My doctors in the UK have provided documentation.

ZOLTAN: Which helps to a certain extent. It's good if you offer us anything you already know: underlying illness, addictions—

MARY-ELLEN: I don't drink at all presently.

ZOLTAN: Sure. The tests will tell us a lot, if we get to that stage. Better to be up-front. We don't want to waste anyone's time.

MARY-ELLEN: You have no reason to doubt a single thing I say.

SENIOR PHYSICIAN: I have a colleague, an anaesthetist. Sorry to interrupt, Zol'—

ZOLTAN: No yes, go ahead—

SENIOR PHYSICIAN: This letter I received—email I received—from this anaesthetist, said, 'Take me off your list'. He won't do altruistic kidneys. 'The donor has nothing to gain and everything to lose.' He says it's against his code.

ZOLTAN: So. *Primum non nocere*. Doing you harm. That's a real question for us.

SENIOR PHYSICIAN: What would you gain from this donation?

MARY-ELLEN: That I don't know.

JUNIOR PHYSICIAN: You don't? Why not?

MARY-ELLEN: It feels right.

SENIOR PHYSICIAN: Would you describe it as an obligation?

MARY-ELLEN: Not at all.

JUNIOR PHYSICIAN: You were Elle Macpherson's publicist.

MARY-ELLEN: I was not.

JUNIOR PHYSICIAN: You weren't?

MARY-ELLEN: I was her brand manager, not PR or publicity or whatever you said. And that was seven years ago. Can't I escape her?

ZOLTAN: Mary-Ellen—

MARY-ELLEN: I had far more important clients than her. I am an intellectual property expert. What has my profession got to do with this?

ZOLTAN: Mary-Ellen.

MARY-ELLEN: Yes?

ZOLTAN: We want to know whether your reactions to stress have been reasonable across your life. Work. Family. All angles. Whether you've had a depressive episode. I want to know whether the stress of the procedure would throw you into crisis.

MARY-ELLEN: It won't.

ZOLTAN: 'Our beginnings never know our ends'.

MARY-ELLEN: T.S. Eliot.
ZOLTAN: That's right.

He sips his Coke Zero.

Why do you want to do this? Just remind me again, would you?

SCENE TWO: A CONFIDANTE OF THE SUPERMODEL

SURTITLE: *'London, boardroom of [redacted].*
              Shortly after 10 a.m. on November 24, 2005'

They are hugging.

ELLE MACPHERSON, *the former supermodel, aged 41, has her arms wrapped around* MARY-ELLEN.

MARY-ELLEN: I'm a little pushed, Elle.

Hugging.

I have a meeting at Claridges.

Still hugging.

You're alright?

  ELLE *shifts the extraordinary locks framing her face. She looks* MARY-ELLEN *in the eye.*

ELLE: No.
MARY-ELLEN: Is it him?
ELLE: No.
MARY-ELLEN: I know that look. It is him. Have you two had words again?
ELLE: Mary-Ellen, no more. This can't go on.
MARY-ELLEN: I can only imagine what you are going through. Divorce can't be easy. But you can trust that British law is the gold standard. Isn't that what they taught schoolgirls like you and me back in Aus? I really must—I want you to call me, alright?

  MARY-ELLEN *is headed for the exit.*

ELLE: It's so sad.
MARY-ELLEN: He's a man. He feels rejected and now he can't bear you being happy.
ELLE: Stop it. Just … I am giving you an opportunity to tell me, M-E. [*'M-E' is a nickname for* MARY-ELLEN.] This is safe, just you and me.

MARY-ELLEN: Tell you what?
ELLE: I love you. This is couched in love.
MARY-ELLEN: I don't go in for all that, Elle.
ELLE: I couldn't do my business without you.
MARY-ELLEN: I know that.
ELLE: You know that.
MARY-ELLEN: Well, yes. I do know that.
ELLE: You're the nuts and bolts of the business and everything I am now.
MARY-ELLEN: Elle, is there something you're trying to tell me?
ELLE: You know what you've done.
MARY-ELLEN: What I've done?
ELLE: I just want you to know first that this is about love.
MARY-ELLEN: Yes, you've said that.
ELLE: You're not a bad person really, Mary-Ellen.
MARY-ELLEN: I'm sorry?
ELLE: It's just so hard to see the unacknowledged.
MARY-ELLEN: This meeting just appeared, just popped up in my diary, telling me to be here in the boardroom. I was told it was about marketing. I'm supposed to be with some rather important clients at Claridges. Tell me what's going on.
ELLE: Well …
MARY-ELLEN: Yes?
ELLE: It's my decision to speak to you alone first. I thought you'd just admit it, M-E. I told myself you would.
MARY-ELLEN: I don't have anything to admit. Are other people coming to this meeting?
ELLE: Some of the partners in the firm.
MARY-ELLEN: Well, I am one of the partners in this firm and you might have an office here but you are our client so—
ELLE: And my lawyer. He is coming too.
MARY-ELLEN: Why?

ELLE digs in her handbag, unfurls a newspaper page.

ELLE: Read it. Have you read it?
MARY-ELLEN: No, I don't tend to read this one.

MARY-ELLEN reads the newspaper.

ELLE: See the date?

ACT ONE

MARY-ELLEN: Yes.
ELLE: See?
MARY-ELLEN: I'm reading—trying to …
ELLE: 'A confidante of the supermodel'?
MARY-ELLEN: Not me. Surely you don't think …
ELLE: There were only two people in those conversations.
MARY-ELLEN: Impossible. Ridiculous. Absolutely. Ridiculous.
ELLE: It wasn't for payment, was it? Because I've made you money.
MARY-ELLEN: I beg your pardon? Really? And I think I've made you a lot of money, Elle. Sorry, but let's be clear.
ELLE: It's possible you don't know you did it.
MARY-ELLEN: No, it's not.
ELLE: Don't feel you're under attack.
MARY-ELLEN: Oh-oh, alright.
ELLE: It's just you don't know you're an alcoholic.
MARY-ELLEN: Have you … have you gone to cloud cuckoo land?
ELLE: M-E, I haven't, I haven't gone there.
MARY-ELLEN: I mean … really … have you ever seen me have a drink?
ELLE: Mary-Ellen, you know I have.
MARY-ELLEN: Once or twice.
ELLE: Please. Come on.
MARY-ELLEN: Elle, I have a bottle of wine a week.
ELLE: Do you?
MARY-ELLEN: Maybe two.
ELLE: Bottles.
MARY-ELLEN: That I share with my husband.
ELLE: If you hadn't been drunk, you wouldn't have been indiscreet. I've told everyone that.
MARY-ELLEN: I'm not the one who's indiscreet, Elle.
ELLE: M-E, you spoke to a journalist.
MARY-ELLEN: I don't know any journalists.
ELLE: It's not until you start doing the little things like taking out your own recycling and you see all the empties and you know avoidance is painful.
MARY-ELLEN: This is stupid.
ELLE: I must not cry anymore. I have to stop crying.
MARY-ELLEN: You're not crying.

ELLE: I want to—cry—because you went to the press about—about my children, Mary-Ellen. About the custody fight. How could you do that?

MARY-ELLEN: No. No. I'm the one protecting you against these things. I got you the office in here for your privacy. That was me, Elle. Protecting you. Naturally all the blokes here wore a hole in the carpet to see a supermodel set up shop in their accounting firm, but it was me getting you that and—

ELLE: [*in French, surtitled*] I am here because I am a businesswoman, not 'The Body'.

MARY-ELLEN: Let's not speak French.

ELLE: [*in French, surtitled*] Why not?

MARY-ELLEN: Because we have to be clear with each other.

ELLE: [*in French, surtitled*] You think I'm not fluent.

MARY-ELLEN: [*in French, surtitled*] It is what you do when you are defensive and think you have to prove yourself.

ELLE: [*in French, surtitled*] I do not live for men to fall in love on me. I am not stupid.

MARY-ELLEN: Do you think I would have dedicated myself to you these last years if I thought that you were?

ELLE: Are you lying to me?

MARY-ELLEN: No.

ELLE: But they're your words, Mary-Ellen. It's your voice. Please just say it.

MARY-ELLEN: Alright … I think the thing to do is get your house swept for bugs, and your cars. I'll book a security firm, a reputable one. Let me do that.

ELLE: Mary-Ellen?

MARY-ELLEN: It'll give you peace of mind because—I can—there's someone from my Conservative Party branch—he's MI5—don't ask me how I know that but—

ELLE: This is crazy. This is subterfuge. You're being crazy. You're lying to me. It's been you all along.

> MARY-ELLEN*'s phone rings.*

MARY-ELLEN: But, Elle, honestly, I'm not me.

ELLE: [*the phone*] That'll be your son. It usually is.

ACT ONE

MARY-ELLEN: What do you mean?

ELLE: You really don't see it, do you?

MARY-ELLEN: It's one of my other clients actually. It's the US Treasury. They don't call me in tears in the middle of the night and ... What I'm saying is: you aren't like these corporations and government clients: all billable hours and—we are friends. I'm good for you and you are good for me and this has been ... fun.

ELLE: I know.

MARY-ELLEN: I really ought to take this call, but let's, you and me, let's sort this out.

ELLE: Let's. Your husband is coming here.

MARY-ELLEN: Why? That's hardly appropriate.

ELLE: Because sometimes it's just as blinding for those who love the addicted person.

MARY-ELLEN: Bruce is going to say how ludicrous this whole thing is.

    MARY-ELLEN *lets her phone ring out.*

ELLE: You sneak off to take calls from your son in meetings.

MARY-ELLEN: So do you. You'll have to leave to collect your boy from school because you sacked another nanny. Nobody brings these things up in a boardroom with men about their children. Why are you saying it to me, Elle?

ELLE: Because I know. We are all carrying wounds.

MARY-ELLEN: Not me.

ELLE: You drink to cover up the guilt of having a disabled child.

MARY-ELLEN: Excuse me? You've never ever even met my son. What are you—are you—?

ELLE: You feel like you couldn't take control when the doctors operated on him when he was an infant. It must have been horrible for you.

MARY-ELLEN: No.

ELLE: It was horrible.

MARY-ELLEN: Yes. But ...

ELLE: You carry the guilt, don't you?

MARY-ELLEN: How is this—how is this at all relevant?

ELLE: There are people who can help; it needn't undo you.

MARY-ELLEN: Can I just say—?

ELLE: Yes, I want you to.

MARY-ELLEN: My son is thirty and, yes, he needs assistance, which I provide for. You have staff. Your children have staff. It's what we do.

ELLE: This has everything to do with that. You wonder if you had intervened and made those doctors hear you—

MARY-ELLEN: Well, hang on, did I say that to you?

ELLE: It's okay to admit it. I love you.

MARY-ELLEN: My son has a job at the TK Maxx store, has for years. I'm proud. He's doing extremely well.

ELLE: You feel guilt and that is okay.

MARY-ELLEN: I'm a little bit speechless here, frankly.

ELLE: You're not.

MARY-ELLEN: No, I'm not, and I may have told you, in confidence, that I did have these awful vibes that I did the wrong thing back then, but please don't you use that against me now. I can prove to you that I did not talk to anyone behind your back, Elle.

ELLE: You can't prove it though, can you?

MARY-ELLEN: No, I suppose because you think because—I mean y'know it seems I did speak to someone but …

ELLE: M-E, thank you. Thank you for progressing just now.

MARY-ELLEN: In what way?

ELLE: We are going to ask you to do something. I know a place and this is what we want to do for you.

MARY-ELLEN: Who is 'we'?

ELLE: I'm not just cutting you off. I don't want people out there saying you can't be trusted. The partners here really really don't want that either.

MARY-ELLEN: Well, I know I haven't done anything.

ELLE: I know a place. It is called The Grove.

MARY-ELLEN: Oh, for goodness sake. The one you went …? I mean. Really? A person like me does not—

ELLE: It's a retreat, a fantastic facility. I want you to stay in my room there.

MARY-ELLEN: 'Celebrity rehab'? My husband will just about die laughing at this. He would if it were funny.

ELLE: It's not though.

MARY-ELLEN: No.

ELLE: It's very serious.

ACT ONE 9

MARY-ELLEN: Yes. I think it might be.
ELLE: You really don't have anything to lose. I am giving you a holiday from the stress. You get to press reset.
MARY-ELLEN: A person like me can't just drop everything. I have clients depending—
ELLE: The partners will take care of that.
MARY-ELLEN: How? They don't know anything about intellectual property. They're just accountants.
ELLE: If we keep this private we can stop it costing you your other clients. Don't make a fuss. My account means a lot to this firm.
MARY-ELLEN: Goodness.
ELLE: This is the pinnacle of your career. And you need your wellness.
MARY-ELLEN: So say I go to this place and convince you I'm not blotto and I, what, 'press reset', and I stride back in here.
ELLE: Yes. We'll be here waiting for you. A private matter. A car will take you to Heathrow on Monday.
MARY-ELLEN: Monday?
ELLE: I'm covering it. We'll arrange everything; flights to Arizona—
MARY-ELLEN: Arizona. On Monday.
ELLE: I need you to do this for me, Mary-Ellen. Please. For me. Will you?

> MARY-ELLEN *thinks it over, gently nods.* ELLE *throws her arms around* MARY-ELLEN.

SCENE THREE: CELEBRITY REHAB

CARL *is in a polo shirt with a holster on his belt.* MARTIN *has a lanyard and a paper cup of pills. They both speak with US accents.*

MARY-ELLEN: You keep away from me.
MARTIN: This is the anxiety, Mary-Ellen.
> SURTITLE: *'The Grove [name changed]'*
MARY-ELLEN: Where I'm from people don't go around with guns. What do you expect?
MARTIN: Carl's here to protect you.
MARY-ELLEN: I am not taking the pills and you can't bloody force me.
MARTIN: You're messaging aggression, Mary-Ellen. Your hand movements, slicing the air.

MARY-ELLEN: When?

Her hands were slicing.

MARTIN: That can be read as very combative.

MARY-ELLEN: What are you on? I am trying to make it clear to you people—

MARTIN: Hey. Hey. We don't need to shriek at each other. Okay?

MARY-ELLEN: Yes. I'm not.

MARTIN: You're a person of conviction, Mary-Ellen. I admire your determination.

He places the medication within reach of her.

You've learnt to cope. You know, y'know what I mean. And I know what happens next. I know the night-sweats, the loss of sleep, yeah, shaking with teeth, teeth chattering—the fear. Your mechanisms will fail. Temptation is unbearable. The medication helps, yeah? That's all.

MARY-ELLEN: No, because I am not going to have withdrawals. I wish you people would listen. I've never even smoked a cigarette in my entire life.

MARTIN: I meet a hell of a lot of people real certain they don't have a problem, Mary-Ellen.

MARY-ELLEN: You want me to cry for you, is that it?

MARTIN: Would you like to cry?

MARY-ELLEN: No.

MARTIN: I cry. Don't mind telling you that. Many mornings, just cry in the shower. Still do that.

MARY-ELLEN: You poor thing.

MARTIN: Nope.

MARY-ELLEN stumbles slightly.

Oops. Okay.

MARY-ELLEN: What? No. I don't know what that was.

MARTIN: Okay.

MARY-ELLEN: No, I just—I just stumbled because I'm usually in heels. That wasn't anything.

MARTIN: Okay. It's alright. Probably your gross motor skills in crisis.

MARY-ELLEN: Please don't be pathetic.

MARTIN: Who?

ACT ONE

MARY-ELLEN: You. You don't make sense.
MARTIN: It's understandable to be confused.
MARY-ELLEN: No, because you people speak in circles.
MARTIN: Do we?
MARY-ELLEN: God.
MARTIN: Okay.
MARY-ELLEN: What?

> DAVID *enters. A sign around his neck reads 'Sex Addict'. He speaks with a US accent.*

MARTIN: Ah … are you …?
DAVID: [*hello*] Hey.
MARTIN: Are you …? What are you looking for?
DAVID: Oh um, a session. A group thing, yeah.
MARTIN: Right. So actually this is not where you need to be.
DAVID: No.
MARTIN: No. This is 5B: 'Mountain Breeze'.
DAVID: Have a look here on my schedule.
MARTIN: No, because 'twelve feet'. Twelve feet at all times for you. You're with Caitlin?
DAVID: Caitlin?
MARTIN: I think your counsellor is—
DAVID: Caitlin. Yeah. Caitlin.
MARTIN: That's meeting room 3C: 'Tranquil Waters'. Do you want Carl to—?
DAVID: [*to* MARY-ELLEN] What are you looking at?
MARY-ELLEN: Sorry.
DAVID: Looking through me?
MARY-ELLEN: No. I'm sorry. I wasn't.
MARTIN: Carl—
DAVID: None of this is my fault.

> DAVID *storms off.*

MARY-ELLEN: Oh, it's never anyone's fault, is it?
MARTIN: Go on.
MARY-ELLEN: This place is ridiculous.
MARTIN: But you agreed to come here, Mary-Ellen, you and your husband. That's a simple fact.

MARY-ELLEN: To keep my job. There are people who wanted me out of the way. I've had time in here to piece this together. I fixed up her contracts.

MARTIN: Who?

MARY-ELLEN: Elle. I improved her percentages and corrected some shocking deals. A lot of the men around her are threatened by me and they got in her ear.

MARTIN: Mary-Ellen, these are exactly the narratives we construct.

MARY-ELLEN: It's the truth.

MARTIN: You said it yourself: let's not blame others.

> MARY-ELLEN *needs something to lean against.*

MARY-ELLEN: I said not to come near me. I'm fine. I don't take drugs.

MARTIN: We don't want you getting hysterical.

> MARY-ELLEN *throws the pills against the wall.*

MARY-ELLEN: I'm not taking the fucking pills.

MARTIN: Mary-Ellen. You have thrown the medication against the wall, is what you've done, okay. I have to take away your privileges.

MARY-ELLEN: Oh, and what are they? Elle made me think this place was like a health spa where I might—I don't know—find Lindsay Lohan on a sunlounge. Doesn't even have proper toilet seats or plugs in the sink. They've told me I can't use the gym or read my books or have my BlackBerry. How can someone kill themselves with a sink plug? What, drown myself? You'd have to be pretty desperate.

CARL: Drown yourself or drink the contents of the sink to get a high.

MARTIN: Thanks, Carl. That's … Mary-Ellen, I'm afraid I have to cancel your morning access to the computer room. We need to limit your obsessive tendencies.

> CARL *retrieves the pills.*

MARY-ELLEN: I'm already in here for Christmas. Do you know what that means for a parent? And I need to keep my husband updated about my health.

MARTIN: We can do that.

MARY-ELLEN: I need to.

MARTIN: You're seeking kindness because you're co-dependent.

> MARY-ELLEN *falls face first into the floor. Comatose.*

Shit. Christ. Shit. Mary-Ellen?

She comes to.

Gee, Mary-Ellen, are you …? How have you managed to get liquor in here?

MARY-ELLEN: No no, I …

MARTIN: We're gonna know; we do your obs.

MARY-ELLEN: No. That's just started to happen.

MARTIN: Falling?

MARY-ELLEN: Yes, falling, just started to happen.

MARTIN: Okay, you need to inform us, things like that. We need to document it.

MARY-ELLEN: No, you don't. Don't.

MARTIN: You're alright?

MARY-ELLEN: Elle and my employer are paying for this place and they will see. They're not to see that.

MARTIN: They'll see that you are making progress by admitting things.

MARY-ELLEN: It's the stress. I am just losing my balance sometimes.

MARTIN: It's the body. It's the withdrawals, your body telling you something.

MARY-ELLEN: But no. It's not. It's simply not that. I was told if I can stick it—stick it out—in this place, then my job will be waiting for me. You mustn't do anything to impinge on that. I'm very good at my job. I'm here to prove them wrong. I am going to prove them wrong.

MARTIN: But you can't, Mary-Ellen. You can't.

SCENE FOUR: AN UPRIGHT CITIZEN

MARY-ELLEN *is outstretched on the floor.*

It's early morning. Her husband, BRUCE, *wanders in from bed towards the kitchen.* BRUCE *has an Australian accent.*

He sees MARY-ELLEN *on the floor. He is carrying a transistor radio. It is on.*

Meanwhile, at the BBC, JOURNALISTS *from Radio 4 are broadcasting from their studio. The radio text found towards the end of this scene is spoken by them under the following dialogue.* BRUCE *turns the radio on and off, providing cut-off points during the scene where indicated.*

SURTITLE: 'BBC Radio 4 'Today' program August 9, 2006 7.04 a.m. [archive confirmed lost]'

BRUCE: Oh.
MARY-ELLEN: I'm fine.
BRUCE: Was it a—?
MARY-ELLEN: No, I'm fine, darling.
BRUCE: Wasn't a hard fall, was it?
MARY-ELLEN: Nope. No. Bruce, have you caught 'Thought of the Day' this morning?
BRUCE: Ah, no, it's coming up.
MARY-ELLEN: I think it's Akhandadhi Das. He's that Vaishnav Hindu teacher and theologian.
BRUCE: Do you need a hand? Getting up.
MARY-ELLEN: No. No, in fact, darling, I think I might like to go for a bike ride today.

BRUCE goes. He takes the radio with him.

Be good to oxygenate. I've got my big list of phone calls to get through.
BRUCE: [*off*] More clients to call?

BRUCE comes back.

Haven't you already—?
MARY-ELLEN: Ones who are yet to get back to me. The loyal old clients. I'm pretty confident. It's just hard to convince people when you're falling flat on your face.

BRUCE turns off the radio.

BRUCE: Mary-Ellen.
MARY-ELLEN: Yes.
BRUCE: You cannot go for a bike ride.
MARY-ELLEN: Yes, I can. In Richmond Park, doing a loop to see the deer again, and you, Bruce, beside me if you like, by my side, Brucie. Precisely what I need.

She cannot bring herself to stand.

The falling happens when I am standing. It happens when I am still. I'm safe on my bike. I'm certain of that.

ACT ONE 15

BRUCE: Eme, you're not a doctor.

'Eme' is BRUCE*'s version of the 'M-E' nickname for* MARY-ELLEN.

MARY-ELLEN: No, and they don't know a jolly thing, do they? Where's the key? To the bike shed.

BRUCE: Not happening. I forbid it.

He turns the radio on again and leaves with it.

MARY-ELLEN: [*calling to* BRUCE] This isn't Her Majesty's Holloway, you know. I'll find the key.

BRUCE: [*off*] You need to rest.

MARY-ELLEN: Oh yes, unemployment sure takes it out of a girl. It's stress. Stress because of the lies and I don't know why I am falling over but I'm not going to …

BRUCE *comes back. He turns the radio down.*

Never mind. I was going to say I'm not going to take it lying down, but that will make you laugh and—

BRUCE: Oh, I see.

MARY-ELLEN: You didn't laugh.

BRUCE: No.

MARY-ELLEN: Brucie, things are going to come our way again. I'm sure of it.

BRUCE: Good for you, Nostradamus.

MARY-ELLEN: He predicted doom and gloom.

BRUCE: Nostradamus on diazepam.

MARY-ELLEN: Take that back.

BRUCE: Sorry.

MARY-ELLEN: No, honestly, fuck you, darling. Say sorry.

BRUCE: Sorry. I did. Sorry.

MARY-ELLEN: I fulfilled my end of the bargain.

BRUCE: Forgive me.

MARY-ELLEN: Week after week in that place and not a single tablet.

BRUCE: You have to forgive me. Eme—

MARY-ELLEN: What am I forgiving you about? Hiding the bike key?

BRUCE: No. Not that. For letting you go to that place.

MARY-ELLEN: That was my fault, not yours. I bet the bike key is in that lovely little leather toiletries case I got you in Rome, where you keep your heart pills.

BRUCE: It's not.
MARY-ELLEN: I'll go look.

She doesn't.

BRUCE: Eme, do you think, if this … Maybe you should think about retirement.
MARY-ELLEN: What? How?
BRUCE: Perhaps that's what this means.
MARY-ELLEN: I'm too young.
BRUCE: I could go back to work.
MARY-ELLEN: You're not doing that. Justin needs you. And you're unwell. How can we afford for me to retire? We can't.
BRUCE: No bike.

He turns the radio up again.

You'll blank out, you'll be mown down by a motor car.

BRUCE *leaves, taking the radio with him.*

MARY-ELLEN: 'Motor car'? Heavens, you're a dag sometimes. 'Motor car'.
BRUCE: [*off*] What's wrong with that?
MARY-ELLEN: I think people have got used to calling them 'cars', Bruce.
BRUCE: [*off*] 'Pushbike'.

BRUCE*'s radio is faintly audible in the next room.*

MARY-ELLEN: What's this about a pushbike?
BRUCE: [*off*] People say 'pushbike' and—
MARY-ELLEN: Yes, but people have 'motorbikes'. I don't think too many people commute in a 'push car'.
BRUCE: [*off*] I'm trying to listen to the wireless.
MARY-ELLEN: [*laughing at him*] 'Wireless'? Goodness me. I love you.

BRUCE *darts back into the room with the radio playing.*

BRUCE: Mary-Ellen, listen.
MARY-ELLEN: Hey?
BRUCE: Sheesh.
MARY-ELLEN: It's 'shish', Bruce, or shoosh.
BRUCE: Sheesh. They mentioned Elle.
MARY-ELLEN: Elle?

They listen to the radio. MARY-ELLEN *manages to stand.*

ACT ONE

BRUCE: Did they …? This is what happened to you.
MARY-ELLEN: I'm calling her.
BRUCE: Calling her?
MARY-ELLEN: I did say those things. They heard my voicemails, Bruce.
BRUCE: On your phone?
MARY-ELLEN: On her phone. They listened to her voicemail. Of course. All of this, all of this because of …
BRUCE: What are you going to say to her?
MARY-ELLEN: I think she owes me an apology, don't you?
BRUCE: I think she deserves a fucking earful. They all do.
MARY-ELLEN: She'll want to apologise. This is horrible.
BRUCE: Sorry means nothing until you get back your clients and reputation back.
MARY-ELLEN: Oh, darling. Look.

She yanks the bike key from BRUCE*'s pyjama pocket.*

Listen for the weather, hon. I want to know what to wear.

BRUCE *turns on the radio. It is midway through a program sting.*

The JOURNALISTS *in their booth throw to the weather man.*

The following radio text is spoken under the previous dialogue. Not all of this material needs to be heard. However, it is crucial that the first mention of 'Elle Macpherson' lands at a point before BRUCE *comments about her.* MARY-ELLEN *and* BRUCE *then listen to that entire report until* MARY-ELLEN *tries to make a phone call.*

STUDIO GUEST: We are seeing increasing concerns. An ever growing number of people are going to want to purchase locally. They're going to be very aware of the carbon emissions which emanate as a result of importing. When one has adequate supply of the same apples or suitable apples locally, it really makes no sense at all and is madness. We are seeing a real determination to sell more English apples and that's got to be immensely good. So there is something of a revival for the English apple, yes. 2005 was a very, very bad year for apple growers worldwide. Prices generally were extremely poor, but we did not see mass grubbing in England as a result of very poor financial returns last year.
BBC RADIO FEMALE HOST: That's pulling up apple trees—'grubbing' … is it?

STUDIO GUEST: Yes. I beg your pardon. Yes. Exactly that. And that, that I think is very significant because it indicates that those who are producing apples are in for the long haul. They've got confidence for the future of the English apple.

BBC RADIO FEMALE HOST: Adrian Barlow from English Apples and Pears, thank you for being with us.

STUDIO GUEST: A pleasure.

BBC RADIO FEMALE HOST: On 'Sharpen Your Memory': forgetting less and remembering more. We ask when and how can we improve our memories. I'll be joined by child psychologist, Tanya Byron; memory athlete, Tony Buzan; and celebrated pianist David Owen-Norris who can play whole sonatas from memory. And we've new insights into our most vulnerable memory—our mental jotting pad or working memory: could understanding its strengths and weaknesses revolutionise childhood learning? That's 'Sharpen Your Memory' tomorrow at nine.

BBC RADIO MALE HOST: It is six minutes past seven. A delegation from the Arab League is on its way to New York to try to get the United Nations to change the Middle East Peace Resolution. Our correspondent there is James Robertson.

BBC CORRESPONDENT: [*on the line*] France and the United States had hoped to bring this to a vote quite quickly: this complex peace plan, which they'd worked on for many weeks. They both feel they have to give an audience, a hearing, to the Arab League delegation. And this afternoon, New York time, the Security Council will hear the three men from the Arab League, on behalf of many Arab countries in the region, present changes—propose changes—to the resolution. In particular they want the council to require Israel to withdraw immediately from southern Lebanon, which isn't in the current, ah, Peace Plan. A special envoy, Tarek Mitri, already in New York, has met with Kofi Annan to explain to him why that is the way forward.

BBC RADIO MALE HOST: But, James, the Israelis are not going to accept that withdrawal. And neither are the United States.

BBC CORRESPONDENT: [*on the line*] That's absolutely right. The Israelis are already saying it is unworkable, that they don't have any faith in the Lebanese armed forces to contain or control Hezbollah.

BBC RADIO MALE HOST: So how do they square the circle, James?

ACT ONE 19

BBC CORRESPONDENT: [*on the line*] Very, very difficult. I think what they'll try to do is to find some new words in the resolution, perhaps an adjective here and there, make some gestures towards the Arab position without frankly any significant changes on the scale Lebanon and the Arab countries want. They simply regard this as a balanced resolution that will suit neither side, please neither side.

BBC RADIO MALE HOST: James, many thanks.

BBC RADIO FEMALE HOST: The disgraced dame returns. After twelve years of self-imposed exile, Dame Shirley Porter has returned to Westminster. Later in the program we visit the sumptuous haunt in Mayfair of the multimillionaire Tesco heiress, who masterminded the gerrymandering operation during the 1980s.

BBC RADIO MALE HOST: Reports have emerged that households as diverse as that of supermodel Elle Macpherson and Clarence House have been eavesdropped by private investigators working for the *News of the World*.

    BRUCE *rushes to* MARY-ELLEN *and makes her listen.*

BBC RADIO FEMALE HOST: Police are investigating three men suspected of intercepting phone messages left by members of the Prince of Wales' staff. The BBC understand further alleged victims of phone interceptions include Liberal Democrat MP Simon Hughes, publicist Max Clifford, football agent Andrew Skylet, supermodel Elle Macpherson, and Gordon Taylor, the chief executive of the Professional Footballers Association.

BBC RADIO MALE HOST: Also known as phone hacking and phone slamming, the method of eavesdropping on a voicemail is as simple as entering the factory-set pin for the mobile phone.

BBC RADIO FEMALE HOST: Further details on that report in the news at the top of the hour.

BBC RADIO MALE HOST: Well, it's August and that means Harrods has begun its 2006 Christmas display. Christmas already? What is the world coming to?

    A radio sting is heard before the following line concludes the scene:

And now the weather ...

    BRUCE *turns the radio off.*

SCENE FIVE: NEWS 1

It torrents. A cascade of news clips (music rather than words, moving images rather than stills):
News of the World *royal editor Clive Goodman and hacker Glenn Mulcaire arrested;*
Andy Coulson, David Cameron's Communications Director, with the new Prime Minister;
Sienna Miller, on her way to court;
The Crown Prosecution Service Director before the media ...

SCENE SIX: WESTMINSTER

It's raining. Within a scramble of umbrellas, MARY-ELLEN *has her arm in a sling. She limps. She plants herself in the path of* CASSANDRA, *an MP.*
SURTITLE: *'Westminster. Five years later ...'*

CASSANDRA: Mary-Ellen?
MARY-ELLEN: We had a meeting.
CASSANDRA: I'm sorry I thought we—
MARY-ELLEN: I didn't get the message. What are you doing now?
CASSANDRA: Mary-Ellen, I'm—we're sitting. Parliament is sitting.

A young man, TOM, *passes.*

This is Tom. Do you know Tom from my office?
TOM: What?
MARY-ELLEN: I had my security pass so I—
CASSANDRA: Brilliant. Yes. I must be in touch with our Putney Heath branch.
MARY-ELLEN: A crime was committed. Five years. Five years, I have made phone calls and written letters. I just want the police to interview me. They say someone will call me back. They never do.
CASSANDRA: I am not ignoring you, Mary-Ellen. Tom will make a time—
MARY-ELLEN: I've given up calling Elle Macpherson. All I want is to be treated with a shred of decency, so I've come to you. You made promises when I first found out.
CASSANDRA: It was pretty limited in Opposition what we could actually do for you.

MARY-ELLEN: We're in government now, Cassandra.

CASSANDRA: Mary-Ellen ... Tom, it's alright, give us a moment. Mary-Ellen, my sense of it is, not now. Phone hacking is sensitive.

MARY-ELLEN: It is when your Communications Chief used to edit *News of the World*. Did the PM ask Andy Coulson if he knew hacking was going on?

CASSANDRA: Look, we are forcing News to do an inquiry.

MARY-ELLEN: Internally? That's a joke. I haven't got my life back. My health, you can see that my health has taken a whack.

CASSANDRA: Been in the wars?

MARY-ELLEN: I have this weird medical condition that they can't diagnose. I fall over.

CASSANDRA: It was courageous—going to rehab.

MARY-ELLEN: They made me. You do know I wasn't a drinker.

CASSANDRA: Oh, I said that. I've said that to people. Y'know, she's fabulous, she's the life of a party, but you can't imagine her sitting at home sinking them back.

MARY-ELLEN: Well no, because I wasn't.

CASSANDRA: I know. That's what I'm saying.

MARY-ELLEN: I was taught in Australia that the UK was the gold standard of the judiciary and democracy.

CASSANDRA: Mary-Ellen, there are some vicious voices screaming out on the left to criminalise tabloid journalism. If the price of a free press is grinning and bearing tits on page three, better that than prescribed stories about how brilliant a carbon floor price is.

TOM: Cassandra, you're—sorry—your ten o'clock is—

CASSANDRA: Yes, good, Tom.

TOM: No, sorry, apparently you are actually late for an interview.

CASSANDRA: Cripes, right—

MARY-ELLEN: Is that it is it? I just go away

CASSANDRA: Mary-Ellen ...

CASSANDRA smiles at her. Goes.

SCENE SEVEN: BLOOD LETTING 1

MARK *waits in a chair, busy on his iPad. He is rigged up for dialysis. A nurse*, SUNITA, *checks some equipment across the room. Other renal patients are seated about, having dialysis.*

SUNITA: Morning, Mark. Skiving off work again?
MARK: Oh yeah. Hiya, Sunita.
SUNITA: We won't keep you plonked there much longer. Promise.
MARK: Pretty used to the dialysis drudgery by now.
SUNITA: Much bleeding this week?
MARK: I had a pretty bad bleed on Friday. I thought maybe I'd have to come back in but it was alright. Lots of blood though.
SUNITA: Always call. Don't want you draining away on us like a sieve, Mark.
MARK: Yeah. Thanks.
SUNITA: 'Oh, he was here before, but now there's just this giant red puddle', kind of thing
MARK: Ha, no, yeah.
SUNITA: Yell out if you need.

> SUNITA *continues on. The patient beside* MARK *opens a takeaway container. The lid breaks as he does so. He is* EMAD.

EMAD: Oh. Broke it.
MARK: I have a plastic bag with my things if you need it.
EMAD: It's alright. I can make do.

> *He offers* MARK *a biscuit from the container.*

MARK: No appetite I'm afraid. Are they …? I know these.
EMAD: Homemade.
MARK: I ate these once before.
EMAD: *Madar*.
MARK: Means 'mother'. You're Iranian. From Tehran?
EMAD: Mahabad.
MARK: More orderly than Tehran. Such neat streets.
EMAD: I've nearly forgotten that I think. Why were you there?
MARK: As a correspondent. I'm a journalist. I was there in 1979.
EMAD: Oh boy.
MARK: Yes.
EMAD: [*the biscuits*] Go on. You and I, our kidneys are dead inside us. What's the worst that can happen? Have a biscuit.

> SUNITA *selects an implement for treatment on this patient—a metal pole. She clubs him over the head.*

SUNITA: [*in Farsi, surtitled*] God is great. Kill the Satanists.

ACT ONE 23

There is blood. The attack is severe.

EMAD: [*in Farsi, surtitled*] The defeat of the Shah was sweet.
SUNITA: [*in Farsi, surtitled*] Clean out Marxist filth.

The bloodied man struggles to chant his slogan.

EMAD: [*in Farsi, surtitled*] The downfall of the Ayatollahs will be sweeter.
SUNITA: [*in Farsi, surtitled*] Death to America's devils.

SUNITA drags the screaming patient.

EMAD: [*in Farsi, surtitled*] The second revolution is coming.

The job done, a trail of blood streaked on the floor, SUNITA *glances at* MARK *with a smile.*

SUNITA: Be with you soon, Mark.
MARK: Thanks. No rush.

As he waits, MARK *sends a tweet.*

MARK: '@maryellenfield Superb interview on BH. Would like to interview you on ABC radio. Please follow me so I can DM'.

SURTITLE: 'Tweet: —@Colvinius January 31, 2011'

SCENE EIGHT: THE DISTRICT LINE

MARY-ELLEN *is among other commuters on the London Tube.*

ANNOUNCEMENT: The next station is Parson's Green.
SECOND ANNOUNCEMENT: This is a District Line train to Wimbledon.
MARY-ELLEN: [*on her phone*] I knew it would be too late to call your time very soon. I'm on the Tube. I thought I had a longer wait at Earl's Court but—
MARK: I'm sorry, who is this?

MARK *is at the ABC Radio studios in Sydney.*

MARY-ELLEN: It is Mary-Ellen Field. From Twitter. You heard my little interview on Broadcasting House.
MARK: Oh. Yes. Hello.
MARY-ELLEN: We're above ground here so the call shouldn't drop out. You threw me with this DM thingo. You're one of these people very *au fait* with the Twitter. It says you have thousands of followers. Tens of thousands.

MARK: It suits me somehow.
MARY-ELLEN: I know you're going to ask me to talk, to talk on your radio program. I need to tell you I can't do that.
MARK: Let's leave it there then.
MARY-ELLEN: I signed an agreement, a compromise agreement, you see, with my former employer, saying I mustn't discuss the reasons I left my job.
MARK: So why did you do the BBC piece?
MARY-ELLEN: Well, I was angry, wasn't I?
MARK: I bet.
MARY-ELLEN: But the real thing is—

> *Daylight goes. The call goes.* MARK *goes.* MARY-ELLEN *sits in silence with other passengers.*

ANNOUNCEMENT: This is Parson's Green.
SECOND ANNOUNCEMENT: Mind the gap between the train and the platform.

> MARY-ELLEN *darts out to the platform.* MARK *is waiting.*

MARY-ELLEN: [*on her phone again*] Me again.
MARK: Hi there.
MARY-ELLEN: I couldn't have you thinking I'm a terribly rude person or something. I want you to know that yes, it was very naughty of me to whisper to the media, and I can tell you I am not the sort who goes about breaching contract, but I hoped people in the Party might hear it.
MARK: Politicians?
MARY-ELLEN: I'm deputy chair of my local Conservative Party branch. Not that it has helped in anyway. I didn't name names in the BBC radio thing. It was only short and I'm very surprised you managed to hear it, actually.
MARK: I keep an ear out. The tabloids and how they operate has been a kind of obsession for me.
MARY-ELLEN: The police have closed the investigation. You know that?
MARK: I saw it, yes.
MARY-ELLEN: They say witnesses won't co-operate. That's a complete lie. I tried for years.

> *Commuters pass her on the platform.*

ACT ONE 25

MARK: Y'know I saw some pretty shoddy foot-in-the-door tactics myself over there. I was the ABC's European Correspondent and there was always that thing of 'How did the tabloids get a lead like that?'

MARY-ELLEN: Yes, like a mosquito bite on Elle Macpherson's bum. That was one of their reports.

MARK: Well, extraordinary access.

   MARY-ELLEN *laughs. She has a terrific laugh.*

You'd have to assume they were tapping phones or paying off cops. Now we know.

MARY-ELLEN: If it weren't for Sienna Miller, an actress who can afford to keep going back to court for the phone records, much of this stuff that's coming out would remain hidden. I'm reading the *Guardian* for the first time in my life.

   MARK *laughs.*

MARK: I should say I am not particularly interested in the celebrity side.

MARY-ELLEN: You're not?

MARK: People are missing the point about the Fleet Street culture. We've been trying to cover phone hacking as best we can at ABC Radio. 'PM' is a nightly current affairs program.

MARY-ELLEN: I know.

MARK: Right.

MARY-ELLEN: I phoned my friend Philip Ruddock about you.

MARK: Ruddock?

MARY-ELLEN: The Attorney-General.

MARK: What did he have to say?

MARY-ELLEN: Well, I think you've been known to give him a mauling over the years.

MARK: Yes. I suspect I have.

MARY-ELLEN: And to his credit he says you're a thoroughly decent person.

MARK: Good grief.

MARY-ELLEN: I am not the type who draws attention to herself: a product of my upbringing—not that I recall my brother ever being contained. I am apprehensive, even talking like this now to a … Journalists are not my favourite people.

MARK: Understandable. People respond to trauma in different ways. Some want to speak. Some don't.

MARY-ELLEN: Yes, well, nobody has ever … / You know I—
MARK: You know I—Sorry, I cut you off.
MARY-ELLEN: No no. That's alright. What were you going to say?
MARK: Ah…
MARY-ELLEN: It has been traumatic, like you say. My health has suffered. The doctors have only just managed to diagnose this thing going on in my brain where my heart forgets to circulate blood. It is a complete nightmare and nobody seems to care. I cut you off again.
MARK: All I was going to say is that I remember, when I was in Brussels, we were to board a ferry. We missed it, y'see. *The Herald of Free Enterprise*. It sunk crossing The Channel.
MARY-ELLEN: I think I remember that on the news.
MARK: One hundred and ninety-three passengers and crew perished.
MARY-ELLEN: And you would have been killed?
MARK: Or a survivor. The point is, at the scene—I went from would-be passenger to reporter, y'see—and some people wanted to speak, they needed that. And I learnt not to force them. So I, ah—
MARY-ELLEN: Would you have spoken, Mark, if you had managed to swim free?
MARK: I, ah, I've never really thought about that. Probably not. No. So, far be it from me to force anyone. Mary-Ellen, I do want phone hacking at the forefront of 'PM', and yes, we need an Australian angle for the show, but we will find another one.
MARY-ELLEN: Rupert owning most of your press not Australian enough?
MARK: It's not the freshest take on it. You could do an interview on the condition of anonymity.
MARY-ELLEN: Yes well, tabloids like *News of the World* run on blind sources, don't they? I have been an unnamed source before, Mark, unwittingly.
MARK: Yes. You have. And it was wrong.

'PM' music sting. Radio broadcast. MARK *is in the studio.*

'You may well have heard about the saga in the UK of Rupert Murdoch's Sunday tabloid the *News of the World* and its widespread hacking of celebrities' phones and voicemail messages. What you may not have heard so much about is the collateral damage to people in the celebrities' orbits.

The majority of the hacking was on voicemail messages with

detectives, paid by Murdoch's company hacking in for juicy details of the celebrities' business or personal life.

One of the celebrities already believed to have received a big compensation payout is the Australian model and underwear magnate Elle Macpherson.

A non-disclosure agreement covers that payout but there's been no vindication or compensation for someone in her circle whose life was ruined by the hacking.'

SURTITLE: *'Mark Colvin reported this story on Wednesday, February 9, 2011, 18:29:00'*

SCENE NINE: BLOOD LETTING 2

CHARON *is a Hutu man with bright mismatched clothing. He holds a machete. His arm is bleeding. He exists in Goma, near Rwanda, in 1994.*

CHARON: [*in French, surtitled*] What are you doing here?
MARK: Pardon?
CHARON: [*in French, surtitled*] Fool. I asked what you are doing here.
MARK: Oh, I am just, ah—
CHARON: [*in French, surtitled*] You have made a mistake coming here.
MARK: Please. Don't—don't come any closer. I'm no threat to you.
CHARON: [*in French, surtitled*] What are you saying? What are you saying to me? Are you ready to die now?
MARK: [*switching to French*] We have bottled water in the truck. We will give you some.

The remainder of the following exchange between MARK *and* CHARON *is in French and surtitled.*

CHARON: I have my stream.
MARK: The water is filthy. We have cans of tuna also. You're injured. I'll give them to you.
CHARON: I don't want your poisonous food.
MARK: I will go. You can go too. The authorities want you to return.
CHARON: What do you know of my authorities?
MARK: I am press. I was told on a satellite phone. The new Rwandan government is calling for refugees to return, civil servants to resume work.

CHARON: If we go back they will pull out our eyes, cut off our hands and chop off our legs.
MARK: Why?
CHARON: I'll only go back with the Interahamwe. Kill or be killed. Even the children. This is eradication.
MARK: Please. Kill me and you remain in this hell with only more uncertainty. Let me go and I can report what is going on here in Goma.

>   CHARON *stands over him.*

CHARON: Because you are clever and white and think you can walk away without even a little scratch. I will give you a scratch, mister.

>   MARK *shields himself.* SUNITA *sees. She is in the renal ward and so is* MARK. *He is on dialysis.*

SUNITA: That uncomfortable?
MARK: Ah…

>   CHARON *has gone.*

SUNITA: Might need adjusting, does it?
MARK: Ah, I think it just …
SUNITA: Oh yes, that's looking a bit … a bit raw there. Let me just … Won't be a minute. You just carry on with what you are doing.

>   MARK *mops his brow.* MARY-ELLEN—*panicked*—*comes to him. She is in London.*

MARY-ELLEN: [*on her phone*] Mark, have I woken you?
MARK: [*on his phone*] Ah, sorry, who is this?
MARY-ELLEN: Mary-Ellen Field. Didn't you save my number?
MARK: Ah yes, hello.
MARY-ELLEN: You sound sick.
MARK: I'm alright. How are you?
MARY-ELLEN: Dreadful. What have we done?
MARK: What's the matter?
MARY-ELLEN: My phone won't stop with journalists calling. I have no idea what to do.
MARK: Why?
MARY-ELLEN: Shit, they'll come to my door. They'll upset the neighbours and who knows what. I've had to take myself to my club in St James to hide.

ACT ONE

A nearby CLUB MEMBER *reads a newspaper and sips a whisky within earshot of* MARY-ELLEN.

MARK: But why are you calling me?

MARY-ELLEN: So you can tell me what to do.

MARK: Well, how was this sparked by our segment?

> SUNITA *returns.* MARK *signals an apology for being on the phone, but she's fine with it. It's all routine.*

MARY-ELLEN: The police are reopening the investigation.

MARK: Because of you?

MARY-ELLEN: No. I can hardly make that claim, but you did embolden me, didn't you, and my former employer hasn't come after me and I just thought, well—I spoke to a few others.

MARK: Which others?

> MARY-ELLEN *turns herself away from the* CLUB MEMBER.

MARY-ELLEN: *New York Times*, the *Guardian*, the *Independent* and CNN. Check online. Even Murdoch's Sky have been calling, but I want it all to stop now. I'd prefer it's just you. I'll just talk to you, Mark.

MARK: Obviously it's in my interests to have you speak exclusively but if I were you, I'd take myself down to somewhere like Abingdon Green outside Parliament. Arrange that you'll give each of them a five-minute interview.

MARY-ELLEN: Do you think that will work?

MARK: It's all they want. And it benefits you to tell it on your terms. It is pretty astonishing watching it all unfold: Andy Coulson's resignation from Downing Street.

MARY-ELLEN: What was David ever thinking, letting him into Number Ten? How could an editor not know hacking was going on? 'One rogue reporter' and … It's just not true.

SUNITA: Okay, that's all good, Mark.

MARK: Thanks, Sunita.

MARY-ELLEN: What's that?

MARK: Sorry, just dealing with—

SUNITA: Moving well.

MARK: Yeah, okay, thanks. Thanks.

> SUNITA *leaves him. The machine purifies his blood.*

MARY-ELLEN: Mark, I'm sorry if I am moaning to you about all this. It can be a bit overwhelming for Bruce.
MARK: Your husband?
MARY-ELLEN: I find myself shielding him from it.
MARK: Yeah, I do some of that.
MARY-ELLEN: With who?
MARK: Oh, I don't know. Family. From time to time. To alleviate worry.
MARY-ELLEN: Bruce cares so deeply. And he's so proud of how hard I worked. Lawyers have started calling us. There are several people heading for High Court civil action apparently. They want our case too. I know I'm a complete nobody but—
MARK: You seem to be bringing on a bit of ruckus.
MARY-ELLEN: Mark, I just don't see how people could be so cruel. Am I delusional?
MARK: Yes.
MARY-ELLEN: What?
MARK: People are cruel, Mary-Ellen. Very. What are you going to do about it?
MARY-ELLEN: Well, I don't know. I suppose I am going to do my own little press conference like you say.
MARK: You do whatever you think is right, Mary-Ellen. Keep me posted.
MARY-ELLEN: Of course I will. What's that noise?
MARK: It's just some equipment where I am.

His blood cycles in the machine.

MARY-ELLEN: You really don't sound too crash hot.
MARK: Feeling better by the minute, actually.

SCENE TEN: AN OLIVE BRANCH

MARY-ELLEN *and* BRUCE *are with their lawyer,* LUCAS.

LUCAS: Well, for News Group, not a bad settlement offer. More than my other non-high-profile hacking clients.
BRUCE: It's an insult.
LUCAS: But it's a sign. They know you're valuable, Mary-Ellen.
MARY-ELLEN: What about loss of income?
BRUCE: My wife was headhunted to her position. Even in a slow year it would be Mary-Ellen given a bonus.

ACT ONE

LUCAS: Completely. We ask for more.
MARY-ELLEN: They only make an offer like this to shut you up.
LUCAS: A win is a win, whether in court or undisclosed, so long as you're justly compensated.
MARY-ELLEN: No. This weasel-worded piece of shit aims to keep the evidence out of the public domain. That's not a win. They claim they'll happily hand over documents 'regarding or concerning the claimant's mobile telephone numbers, pin numbers …' la la la.
BRUCE: And don't we want that stuff?
MARY-ELLEN: They don't have it. My phone was never hacked. They know that. It was Elle's. So what other things are they hiding?
LUCAS: Probably a lot. But rejection of a settlement exposes you if we go to court. If we lose or get damages of even a penny less than their offer, you could be liable for the defendant's costs.
MARY-ELLEN: I'm aware of that.
BRUCE: I wasn't.
MARY-ELLEN: Darling, it's only if the judge grants a costs order. That would be outrageous. We know from prior court cases that Mulcaire kept copious notes when he was listening to voicemails. And now the police are finally doing their job, you can bet more evidence will surface. I'm rightly seeking justice; that's what the courts are for. And my actions help other victims.
LUCAS: News Group will stall. Familiar tactics. They'll paper my office with documents that I'm obliged to read in full.
MARY-ELLEN: Is a settlement in your interest? Just say so.
LUCAS: I want a win. I'll go to court. But I will remind you of their ferociousness. They will use everything in their arsenal against you.
BRUCE: There is your health, Eme. I'm not the only one with the dicky heart.
MARY-ELLEN: Oh, I'm alright.
BRUCE: Your heart stops beating sometimes.
MARY-ELLEN: You're making it sound worse than it is. Doesn't stop; it speeds up. [*To* LUCAS] Messages from the brain to the heart. I've had this procedure: a little appliance stitched in that keeps my rhythm in check. You ought to see me dance. To The Kinks. He hates it.
BRUCE: I love it, I love nothing more than watching you dance.
MARY-ELLEN: [*to* LUCAS] I was collapsing and of course everyone just thought I was trollied.

LUCAS: That's exactly the sort of thing they'll use against you: the accusations against your character.
MARY-ELLEN: That are not true.
LUCAS: There are ways to mitigate these perceptions. Even what you wear can—
MARY-ELLEN: I'll look professional, but I'm not wearing a grey pants suit. This is me. I know who I am.
LUCAS: You went to rehab, Mary-Ellen.
MARY-ELLEN: Who do you think locked me up—the fashion police?
BRUCE: It was so she'd keep her job.
MARY-ELLEN: Actually they tried this in The Grove: made the models wear their clothes inside out, so as not to draw attention to themselves, which had the complete opposite effect, especially from the sex addicts—the great majority of whom were lawyers, by the way.
LUCAS: The other perception is that you talk too much.
MARY-ELLEN: Right. Alright. Prattle a little bit too much, do I?
LUCAS: I apologise for that.
MARY-ELLEN: Saying I'm 'gobby'?
LUCAS: Yes—no.
MARY-ELLEN: Not the first time this 'sheila' has heard it. Go ahead, what is it you have to say?
LUCAS: I want to suggest we make a counter offer to settle for over a million pounds.
MARY-ELLEN: I see.
BRUCE: Well. That's a good figure.
LUCAS: We can reasonably point out to them that in due course the documents relating to Elle Macpherson will throw light on the full extent of their actions and the losses caused.
MARY-ELLEN: Mmm.
BRUCE: Mary-Ellen and I planned to slip across to friends in France. Even though the belt's a bit tight at the minute, I think we should. We can take the time to think this through.
LUCAS: They'll want a prompt response.
MARY-ELLEN: Do you think they'll knock it back?
LUCAS: I'm getting good traction on settlements. It'll be a decent sum.
MARY-ELLEN: I forgo my day in court.
BRUCE: And this whole thing is over and done.

ACT ONE

LUCAS: You forgo their intimidations. I don't go about sharing this, but my daughter was followed. We spotted a guy filming her. She's fourteen.

BRUCE: Goodness me.

LUCAS: Police have confirmed it. He's the same geezer I found going through our bins and filming me on my way to work. They don't like me taking them on, gathering victims like yourself. How long until they do that type of thing to you?

MARY-ELLEN: Yeah. What you're telling me makes me think they already are.

BRUCE: In what way?

MARY-ELLEN: I took my computer to the Apple shop. The young lads there couldn't explain these error messages I was getting. And then something my journalist friend, Mark Colvin, sent me ended up on our son's Facebook.

BRUCE: Why didn't I know that?

MARY-ELLEN: Apple confirmed that there'd been tampering from an outside source.

LUCAS: They put that in writing?

MARY-ELLEN: Just spoke to me—at the Genius Bar.

BRUCE: Mary-Ellen?

LUCAS: Take your laptop to the police. I want these things documented.

MARY-ELLEN: Bruce, I didn't want you to be alarmed ... but the other day you were on Putney High Street and I was in the bath at home reading my papers ... my mobile telephone dialled your number. Just called you.

BRUCE: I'm not sure they could do that.

MARY-ELLEN: I saw it.

LUCAS: It's worth checking, honestly.

BRUCE: Mary-Ellen—

MARY-ELLEN: I didn't want you to think I was a nutter.

BRUCE: When have I ever thought that?

MARY-ELLEN: I have. I've been made to question my sense of things.

BRUCE: Eme, you mustn't keep things from me. Never. Tell me everything.

MARY-ELLEN: I will.

BRUCE: Thank you, yes.

MARY-ELLEN: The other day I saw this one chap—

BRUCE: There's more?
MARY-ELLEN: Just this. He's not in the trench coat and glasses or anything, but I swear I saw this man in three different places across London. Staring at me. I know it. I know they are trying to frighten me.
LUCAS: It works for them.
BRUCE: And we have this opportunity to put it to bed.
MARY-ELLEN: No. This is exactly what I want people to know about. I want people to see what they do. I want my day in court.

SCENE ELEVEN: SYSTEM CRASH

MARY-ELLEN *is at home in London.* MARK *is in Sydney in the studio. They are recording a radio interview.*

MARK: 'Against that background, then, how do you regard the revelations of the last few days about how close many of those very senior police were with News Limited, News International?'

> SURTITLE: *'Mark Colvin "PM" program, ABC Radio, Monday, July 18, 2011 18: 19: 00'*

MARY-ELLEN: [*on her phone*] 'Oh well, it's just unbelievable. I mean, you know we had those—all those years ago in Sydney and then in Melbourne—with interesting behaviour by the police. But this is extraordinary. When Rebekah Brooks said in the Commons Select Committee—2003, I think it was—that they did pay policemen and then changed her mind later on, it seems the police seem to have been earning more money from bribes from the *News of the World* than they were from their own pay packets. It's unbelievable.'

MARK: 'Sir Paul Stephenson, the head of Scotland Yard, has resigned saying—'

His walking stick falls with a thud.

Oh shit, sorry. I dropped my—

He strains to pick it up. He can't.

Shit. God. [*To a producer via mic*] Can you send someone in please?
MARY-ELLEN: Ah ... what do you mean?
MARK: Sorry, Mary-Ellen, my walking stick rolled off the desk, so we're going to have to go again.
MARY-ELLEN: Oh, that's fine—

MARK: [*to a producer via mic*] Yes please. And is he getting my water? No, I've drunk it all. And could you—actually—I want something to mop my brow. I'm sweating on my papers.

MARY-ELLEN: It's winter there.

MARK: Pardon?

MARY-ELLEN: I hope I haven't got you out of your sickbed. I didn't want to be interviewed by anyone else so I waited for you to get back from your holiday.

MARK: Not a holiday, a prison stint. I was in hospital.

MARY-ELLEN: Oh, you should have said.

MARK: I'd far prefer to be at work. We're just waiting for …

MARY-ELLEN: What's that?

MARK: [*to colleagues via mic*] Well, how long's …? Really? Mary-Ellen—

MARY-ELLEN: Yes?

MARK: I have people speaking in my cans.

MARY-ELLEN: Cans?

MARK: Earphones. We're just waiting for— Are you alright waiting on the line?

Silence.

Mary-Ellen?

MARY-ELLEN: Oh. Yes. I'm here.

MARK: Apologies to make you—

MARY-ELLEN: No yes, it's fine.

MARK: Perhaps I should call you back. We've had a system crash. [*To colleagues via mic*] Jo, I'm going to rest on the couch until you've … Yeah. Not really, but I'll be— I just want to rest until it's sorted out. Where is Kane with my water? Would you mind telling him to hurry back from the well or whatever he's doing about it?

MARY-ELLEN: Is the walking stick because of your hips, Mark?

MARK: Ah … just a minute.

MARY-ELLEN: Sorry.

KANE, *a cadet, brings* MARK *water and tissues for his brow.*

MARK: Thanks, Kane. And, mate, you need to redo your piece. 'Strunk and White' is waiting on my desk for you. That was embarrassing. Really.

KANE *thanks him and goes.*

The ankle is pretty bung too.

MARY-ELLEN: Are you speaking to me?

MARK: Yes.

MARY-ELLEN: It's reporting the Rwandan genocide that did this to you.

MARK: Well. Sort of. It started there.

MARY-ELLEN: I googled you.

MARK: Right. Well, I'm a pretty open book.

MARY-ELLEN: Are you? Kept a lot of it under your hat.

MARK: We drove south towards Goma and we could see little bundles by the side of the road, and we were wondering what they were. They were just side by side for the last probably twenty or thirty kilometres, side by side on both sides of the road—death—corpses everywhere.

MARY-ELLEN: I'm being terribly nosey.

MARK: I could hardly object given I am about to interview you.

MARY-ELLEN: Oh, yes.

MARK: I picked up a mysterious disease and they pumped me full of so much cortisone that my joints turned to chalk. Something called avascular necrosis.

MARK *gets himself to the couch.*

MARY-ELLEN: You ought to get to Spain, Mark. They have a much better system for organ donation than Australia. You'd get a new kidney right away.

MARK: Yeah. Three hours down the highway to visit Mum is about as far as I get. And that's only when Canberra Hospital can take me in for dialysis. I'm not complaining.

MARY-ELLEN: No, of course. Canberra's very … Wonderful trees. Mark, you wanted to get off the phone.

MARK: It's alright. I'm reclining now like Mars in that Sandro Botticelli—

MARY-ELLEN: The spent warrior.

MARK: Ha. In my dreams.

MARY-ELLEN: I was at the National Gallery this week. Bruce and I are members there and the Portrait Gallery and the Royal Academy.

MARK: I spent countless hours in all of them—years ago. It was the Rembrandts that really knocked me over.

MARY-ELLEN: Mmm. Me too.

ACT ONE

MARK: The self portraits where you see him going from a young vigorous man—you can see what I'm getting at—then staring into his older eyes, so much etched across his face. The various disappointments, loss. All of it. He's so unsparing. When I was stationed at our Belgium bureau I had the Musée des Beaux Arts down the road. Have you been?

MARY-ELLEN: I haven't. It's the one W.H. Auden wrote the poem about.

MARK: Yes, that's it.

MARY-ELLEN: I imagine you miss it, the travel.

MARK: God, I'm really boiling up. I'm feeling very dry.

MARY-ELLEN: Oh, go. Do you need to?

MARK: Think I'll be alright. It's weird though. You asked whether I miss it, the travel. I do. Even my childhood was spent roaming the globe.

MARY-ELLEN: And now a radio booth.

MARK: Well, I started my career in radio so—

MARY-ELLEN: Oh, I didn't mean it's—it's not a consolation prize or …

MARK: I think of my radio program as a set of eyes on the world. It's also meant that, as a parent, I've been more present than my own distant father.

MARY-ELLEN: Distant in what way, Mark?

MARK: Outer Mongolia. We were to finally live in the same city when I got into Oxford but he accepted the posting. He was in the British Foreign Service.

MARY-ELLEN: Probably a spy, Mark. A lot of them were MI6.

MARK: Yeah, well that came out later.

MARY-ELLEN: Truly?

MARK: Yes. Mary-Ellen, they are telling me the system is cactus. We're going to need to reschedule, but I'm not available tomorrow.

MARY-ELLEN: Where will you be?

MARK: Hang on, they're talking to me again. [*To the mic*] Jo, not an ambulance please, I'll drive myself.

MARY-ELLEN: I don't know who Jo is, but I think he or she might be right. Go in an ambulance.

MARK: The thing with ambulances—when I broke my thigh bone in 2009 they took me to RPA. When you've got a rare disease it's much better to go to the hospital where your specialists are.

MARY-ELLEN: Will you keep me updated about you, how you are?

MARK: Why?

MARY-ELLEN: Because I'll want to know. I'll be worried about you.

MARK: Really? Don't be.

MARY-ELLEN: 'About suffering they were never wrong,
   The Old Masters: how well they understood
   Its human position; how it takes place
   While someone else is eating or opening a window or just walking dully along …'

MARK: The Auden. You know it by heart.

MARY-ELLEN: No, I'm reading it from my iPhone.

SCENE TWELVE: NEWS 2

NEWS CLIPS:
   Rebekah Brooks and Rupert Murdoch hounded by photographers;
   Milly Dowler's 'missing' notice;
   the Dowler family address the media.

SCENE THIRTEEN: SAINT FELIX'S FINGER BONE

SURTITLE: 'Saint-Félix-Lauragais Parish Church, France'

MARY-ELLEN *lights a candle and prays. A nearby* PARISHIONER *is knelt at a pew.* MARY-ELLEN *sends a text:*

SURTITLE: 'Are you OK?'

The text message hangs in the air without a reply.

SURTITLE: Text message sent by Mary-Ellen Field July, 2011.

MARY-ELLEN *bows her head in prayer. Then, her phone rings loudly in the stone cavern. The* PARISHIONER *groans.* MARY-ELLEN *answers it.*

LUCAS: [*on his phone*] Hello, Mary-Ellen.

   Her lawyer's voice echoes. He is in London.

They're applying for an adjournment.

MARY-ELLEN: [*on her phone*] What? Wait. Can't speak.

   She disconnects the call. LUCAS *exits.* MARY-ELLEN *smiles an apology to the* PARISHIONER.

   SURTITLE: 'Tweet: 'I happened to be awake when James
         Murdoch closed [News of the World]'

ACT ONE 39

MARY-ELLEN *sends a text:*

SURTITLE: *'@Colvinius July 7, 2011. You should be asleep, not tweeting'*

MARK *is in a hospital gown, in Sydney.*

SURTITLE: *'These are the actual text messages between Mary-Ellen Field and Mark Colvin July, 2011'*

SURTITLE: *[Mark] 'This Dowler story is just jaw-dropping'*

SURTITLE: *[Mary-Ellen] 'I worry about you all the time'*

SURTITLE: *[Mark] 'I'd like to tell you I'm fine … Dialysis failed. Back in hospital for yet another op. Not my week.'*

SURTITLE: *[Mary-Ellen] 'Am in the medieval church in Saint-Félix drinking in the incense. Have lit you a candle and am sending you the most positive thoughts. Stay strong.'*

PARISHIONER: [*in French, surtitled*] Annoying.

SURTITLE: *[Mark] 'I'm not at all religious but I do appreciate the thought'*

SURTITLE: *[Mark] 'It's so hard to get good sleep here. Slept 10 pm to 2.30 am, woke & couldn't sleep for 2 hours, slept 4.30-6.30, woken by bright lights flickering, the unannounced phlebotomist unceremoniously sticking needles into me.'*

SURTITLE: *[Mary-Ellen] 'Bon courage'*

The text message surtitles go. MARK *has gone. Time to pray again—but her phone rings!*

MARY-ELLEN: [*on her phone*] Shit shit.
LUCAS: [*on his phone*] Hiya.

LUCAS *has appeared.* MARY-ELLEN *retreats to a small room in the church.*

MARY-ELLEN: [*whispering*] What is it?
LUCAS: Where are you?
MARY-ELLEN: I'm in a … Oh God, I'm in a confessional.
LUCAS: A what?

MARY-ELLEN: I'm in a confessional talking to my lawyer. My mother always told me I'd be struck down by God if I went into a Catholic Church. Tell me she wasn't right. What's this about an adjournment?

LUCAS: They were trying to have us struck out before we began; must have been confident. Now they want to adjourn the hearing that they instigated.

MARY-ELLEN: Why?

LUCAS: Your guess is as good as mine.

MARY-ELLEN: They're floundering, aren't they?

Unbeknownst to MARY-ELLEN, *a* PRIEST *approaches.*

LUCAS: Well, they have grasped what I'm capable of. Have you seen Rebekah Brooks has just resigned as CEO?

MARY-ELLEN: She resigned?

LUCAS: Could be prison next—straight to the tower like a red-headed Rapunzel.

MARY-ELLEN: They're frightened. They want an adjournment because finally the police, the politicians—the people—are all against them and they never thought that could happen. But hack a murdered schoolgirl's telephone? This is actually it. It's the end of Murdoch's reign.

The PRIEST *genuflects. He sits opposite* MARY-ELLEN *behind a grille.*

LUCAS: Hollywood has started calling, which is rather amusing. There are discussions as to which actor will play me in a film.

PRIEST: [*in French, surtitled*] Are there two of you in there?

MARY-ELLEN: Oh, Christ.

LUCAS: They'll fess up for you now, Mary-Ellen.

MARY-ELLEN: [*in French, surtitled*] Bless me, father, for I have sinned.

LUCAS: Sorry, what?

PRIEST: [*in French, surtitled*] What is that other voice?

MARY-ELLEN *can't work out how to turn her phone off.*

LUCAS: We just don't want News forcing you into submission with fucking costs.

PRIEST: [*in French, surtitled*] Are you speaking on a phone in there?

MARY-ELLEN: [*in French, surtitled*] No, I was just—

PRIEST: [*in French, surtitled*] This is a sacred place.

LUCAS: It's a bad line.
PRIEST: [*in French, surtitled*] We have Saint Felix's finger bone in our altar.
LUCAS: I'll be in touch.

The call ends. LUCAS *goes.*

MARY-ELLEN: Oh, thank God.
PRIEST: [*in French, surtitled*] You're English.
MARY-ELLEN: [*in French, surtitled*] Australian actually.
PRIEST: [*in French, surtitled*] Loudmouth drunkards, sly beauties and thieves; I know your sins already.

SURTITLE: 'This encounter with a priest never happened'

SCENE FOURTEEN: OUTSIDE OF JUSTICE

A QC, in a robe with a trolley of court files, cuts a path. His footsteps echo loudly in this legal cathedral. A SECURITY GUARD *marshals people through a scanner gate.*

SURTITLE: 'Her Majesty's High Court of Justice, London'

MARY-ELLEN *is at the front entrance on her phone.* LUCAS *finds her. He taps her arm.*

MARY-ELLEN: Sorry, in a minute.
LUCAS: I really need to talk to you before we go back in.
MARY-ELLEN: Won't be a— [moment.] Just trying to let my friend Marko know the good news. He hasn't been on Twitter for days, but I won't let it worry me until I— Bum-bum, rang out.
LUCAS: Let me deal with media.
MARY-ELLEN: Oh no I give him leads all the time.
LUCAS: Don't. That's my job.
MARY-ELLEN: We talk every day. Marko's going to absolutely love the good news.
LUCAS: 'Good news'? There is no good news today.
MARY-ELLEN: You saw Justice Vos go them. They pretended they lost the files on their computer. Getting so desperate.
LUCAS: Are you focussed on this or busy texting some media mate?
MARY-ELLEN: Actually a dear friend.
LUCAS: Please just stay with me on this. Without that evidence we have no case.

MARY-ELLEN: They can't—can't just defy a disclosure from a judge on the Queen's bench.

LUCAS: Can't they? They just did.

MARY-ELLEN: With a software error?

LUCAS: You watch them say their files can't be restored.

MARY-ELLEN: But if you or I just chopped up evidence we'd be locked up.

LUCAS: Clearly we are not them. We're not Murdoch. And his men want to exhaust you and embarrass and break you.

MARY-ELLEN: But this place is supposed to be the gold standard of justice.

LUCAS: You cannot pretend this isn't happening. The onus of proof is on you. You made the claim. Either we withdraw or we get corroborating testimony.

MARY-ELLEN: Whose?

LUCAS: 'Habeas Corpus'. Get me 'The Body' in court.

MARY-ELLEN: Oh that's neat.

LUCAS: Find a way. Elle said she loved you, didn't she? She put that in writing. We haven't thought about that strategy yet, appealing to her as a person.

MARY-ELLEN: Yes I, well I can, I can call her—again.

LUCAS: Go heart to heart. A chance for her to be the good guy. Let me know how you go.

> LUCAS *leaves her.* MARY-ELLEN *looks at her phone. She dials a number. People walk around her. A voice answers, in Sydney.*

MICHELE: [*on her phone*] Hello.

MARY-ELLEN: [*on her phone*] Yes. Hello. I'm, um, I'm trying to reach Mark Colvin.

MICHELE: Who is this?

MARY-ELLEN: Mary-Ellen Field.

MICHELE: Who?

MARY-ELLEN: A dear friend of Mark's. Is he there?

MICHELE: He can't answer his phone right now.

MARY-ELLEN: Why not?

MICHELE: Ahh … beg your pardon?

MARY-ELLEN: I want to know he is alright.

MICHELE: He's, yes … he is surrounded by those who love him.

MARY-ELLEN: Are you telling me …?

ACT ONE 43

MICHELE: I need his phone for family; in case they call. Your number has been phoning a lot. You understand?
MARY-ELLEN: Just ... I love him. Tell him that.
MICHELE: Sorry, how do you know him?
MARY-ELLEN: Well, from his radio program really.
MICHELE: Oh.
MARY-ELLEN: We're like old-fashioned pen pals.
MICHELE: Okay, look I don't know how you got this number but—
MARY-ELLEN: Mark gave it to me. Do you work with him?
MICHELE: I'm his wife.
MARY-ELLEN: Oh, he's never even mentioned your name; I don't know it. He didn't ... I'm sorry, that must sound terrible.
MICHELE: You mustn't call this number again.

The call is terminated. MARY-ELLEN *looks at her phone. She goes to the security screening. She places the phone in a plastic tub. She takes off her shoes. She watches her stuff convey away. She waits to go through.*

MARY-ELLEN: 'Dear Mark, there is something I need to do for you. I believe I was put on this earth to do it.'

SURTITLE: 'This correspondence has since been lost'

MARY-ELLEN *walks through the scanner. The* GUARD *watches for the indicator to light up.* MARY-ELLEN *is free to proceed.*

SCENE FIFTEEN: THE OFFER

MARY-ELLEN *sits by an empty bed in Prince of Wales Hospital, Sydney.* MARK *shuffles towards the room with a drip and his walking stick. He is dressed in a hospital gown. He is gravely ill.*

MARY-ELLEN: Mark. Hello, Marko.
MARK: What are you doing here?

END OF ACT ONE

ACT TWO

SCENE ONE: THE OFFER (CONTINUED)

MARY-ELLEN: I've been all around this decrepit maze.
MARK: I shouldn't be too hard to catch.
MARY-ELLEN: So good to finally be with you, Mark.

>   MARY-ELLEN *moves in to kiss him.* MARK *is thrown.*

MARK: Ah, yeah, yep. Hi.

>   *She kisses his cheek.*

Sorry, I'm clammy.

>   *She wipes his sweat from her lips.*

Would you prefer—? I think it's better not in my room.
MARY-ELLEN: I'm happy here. You'll be more comfortable.
MARK: Really? I probably pong.
MARY-ELLEN: Just hospital. I can open a window.
MARK: They're bolted.
MARY-ELLEN: Certainly due for an upgrade.
MARK: They're very good here.
MARY-ELLEN: Bit awful though. Do you know my parents were married at Saint Jude's up the road? A good omen.
MARK: The patron saint of lost causes?
MARY-ELLEN: You don't believe in smells and bells so it's irrelevant. How's your family?
MARK: Oh, y'know, been a bit touch and go, the septicaemia.
MARY-ELLEN: You don't look at all good, Mark. Not yourself.
MARK: You've just met me.
MARY-ELLEN: I've seen photographs. Do they know I'm here, your family?
MARK: Should they?
MARY-ELLEN: You've been very rude, Mark. You haven't replied to my offer.

>   *Silence.*

ACT TWO

A job has never lured me back to Australia and now out of the blue—only temporary but more than a bit spooky. The coin is nice too with Murdoch's lawyers stalling to ratchet up my costs. You'll be seeing a lot of me, Mark.

MARK: Oh well, that's good.

Silence.

MARY-ELLEN: Rebekah Brooks has to face court.

Silence.

MARK: Mary-Ellen, I cannot possibly accept your offer.

MARY-ELLEN: I expected you might say that. All my reading tells me it is often very difficult for the recipient to accept the gift.

MARK: Please. Let me talk.

MARY-ELLEN: Are you cranky with me or the pain?

MARK: I am not … cranky. You must understand, I would never, never, allow you to put your own health at risk. Besides, it's illegal. A stranger cannot donate a kidney.

MARY-ELLEN: But, Mark, I am not a … [stranger.]

MARK: They'd think you were coerced.

MARY-ELLEN: Well I can easily prove otherwise. I've kept it all: every email and tweet and whatever—SMS.

MARK: Really? Why?

MARY-ELLEN: We're like soul mates.

MARK: That's a pretty weird claim to make. I'm sorry if you've misunderstood, if I came across as … rude.

Silence.

MARY-ELLEN: I … I've brought you something … I thought, ah …

She lifts a heavy bag from near her feet.

Y'know I found these old plates—1820—in the Salvos shop in Wandsworth. I sent a photo to you.

MARK: Yes, I remember.

MARY-ELLEN: And you loved them.

MARK: You brought them all this way for—

MARY-ELLEN: For your mother. Not for you.

MARK: No I know because—

MARY-ELLEN: You both loved them. I knew you would. Had to take them as carry-on.

MARK: Gosh.
MARY-ELLEN: For your mother for Christmas.
MARK: Well, I'll be paying you for this.
MARY-ELLEN: No, you won't.
MARK: I can't have it; you lugging them all this way.
MARY-ELLEN: Wasn't any extra.

She unwraps one of the plates.

Oh dear, I think …
MARK: It is most kind.
MARY-ELLEN: Oh dear I think this one is … Oh this one is smashed.
MARK: Never mind.
MARY-ELLEN: Oh, that's such a … I was so careful.
MARK: We can glue it.
MARY-ELLEN: I hope the others are …
MARK: I'm really touched. I am. Mum will love them.
MARY-ELLEN: Such a shame if I've gone and brought you a bag of smashed-up dust. Where do you want to …?
MARK: Wherever you think. There.
MARY-ELLEN: Unpack them gingerly, you'll end up lacerating yourself.
MARK: I should have written to you.
MARY-ELLEN: Yes. You should have, Mark.
MARK: I am grateful for your offer.
MARY-ELLEN: I've done all the research; the risk to me is tiny.
MARK: I cannot ask this of you.
MARY-ELLEN: You haven't asked me to do a thing; this is completely my choice. I've been off my HRT for months. That's Hormone Replacement Therapy for menopause.
MARK: Why are you off that?
MARY-ELLEN: I overhauled everything I do. And my diet. My doctors have been very supportive.
MARK: I'm astounded you would; you never discussed it with me.
MARY-ELLEN: Didn't want to get your hopes up. We're the same blood type y'know. If that's not a sign I don't know what—
MARK: How on earth do you know that?
MARY-ELLEN: Because I told you a story about asking my mother if she was Rhesus negative like me and she went completely bonkers, as though I might find out she's not actually my mother, which might

have suited me—and you said, 'Isn't that amazing I am also A neg'—or words to that effect. It's very rare. So there was that bit of sleuthing.
MARK: Well it's a tad more involved than blood types—
MARY-ELLEN: I know. I know. And if they tell us we're incompatible then away I'll go but I'm certain that won't happen. I have tremendous vibes about all this.
MARK: We are incompatible. I interviewed you. I'm a journalist and you're asking me to betray my ethics.
MARY-ELLEN: You've been on dialysis for years. It could be decades. Let me help you.
MARK: When I interview a person I do not profit from them. And there are laws in this country to ensure when a person donates a kidney they don't profit either.
MARY-ELLEN: You need to fact-check that one. I don't want anything from you. Altruistic donation from a living person is ideal. My kidney's only got to scoot across a hallway, not be pickled on a plane from the outback or somewhere, sitting there deoxygenating and, and, and encased, before that, y'know, in the decaying flesh of some corpse.
MARK: Please. I'm really not feeling the best today, so it wouldn't be good to argue about this with me.
MARY-ELLEN: No. No, it's not that, Mark. You just don't want a woman to go the whole nine yards for you.
MARK: Mary-Ellen, what have you got into your head?
MARY-ELLEN: You clearly don't tell your lovely wife a thing.
MARK: I beg your pardon?
MARY-ELLEN: She didn't even know I existed.
MARK: Why are you speaking to her?
MARY-ELLEN: Mark, I know what men are like who came out of those posh boarding schools. You've told me. You were ill as a child, lonely as a child, and—
MARK: What do you presume to know about me?
MARY-ELLEN: I know things we have shared. Didn't your mother have to come and speak to your schoolmaster because she saw scars on your legs? Beaten and tormented by the thugs that purported to be teachers.
MARK: Laying it on a bit thick.
MARY-ELLEN: Shivering at night.
MARK: Did I tell you that?

MARY-ELLEN: Wondering where in the world Father was with all his secrecy making you guess how much he truly loved you and I think he loved you very much.

MARK: Oh please.

MARY-ELLEN: You're scared you'll be beholden to me so you're shutting me out. Posting yourself to outer Mongolia. Yes you make yourself publicly available to so many people but when it comes to the crunch you can't bear to do that privately and I'm not having it. There. Does that sound like a stranger? I know you.

MARK: I don't want to have to say this to you, Mary-Ellen, but the real reason you made your offer had nothing to do with me and everything to do with you and the cruel things that have beset you. And I am sorry that is the case. I feel deeply about what you have been through. But it will not heal that ordeal to pursue some fantasy of being my saviour.

MARY-ELLEN: Alright then. Are you ready to die?

MARK: This discussion has ended. You are not to mention it to me or anyone else—and certainly not my family. Now if you don't mind I need to empty my pee and then I've got more fucking dialysis.

She watches him lumbering away from her.

SCENE TWO: DARLING HARBOUR

BRUCE *appears, in London.* MARY-ELLEN *is in Sydney's Darling Harbour. This is a phone call.*

BRUCE: [*on his phone*] Eme?

MARY-ELLEN: [*on her phone*] Brucie Bruce.

BRUCE: Happy to hear from me?

MARY-ELLEN: I am. I'm so far away.

BRUCE: Where are you?

MARY-ELLEN: Darling Harbour. Isn't government stupid? They're about to dismantle that hopeless monorail.

BRUCE: Justin's got Employee of the Month.

Silence.

You there?

MARY-ELLEN: Yes.

ACT TWO

BRUCE: You alright?
MARY-ELLEN: Yes. That's wonderful. Tell him, 'Mum's proud, so very proud'.
BRUCE: Well, he's lying here on the couch like Lady Muck and he's got a plate of Vegemite toast.
MARY-ELLEN: I wish I could see him.
BRUCE: We oughta work out this Skype bizo. I tell you he doesn't look like 'Employee of the Month' from where I'm standing. Employee of Bush Week. He's laughing.
MARY-ELLEN: How many is it now?
BRUCE: What's that?
MARY-ELLEN: Times he has been Employee of the Month at TK Maxx?
BRUCE: Nineteen.
MARY-ELLEN: Well. Goodness me.
BRUCE: You are alright, aren't you?
MARY-ELLEN: Just … I miss you all. I'm not home to do his special dinner. Do him a cake.
BRUCE: He said he wants toast.
MARY-ELLEN: Bruce, do him my carrot cake. The recipe is there in the— the book is probably on that stand on the bench, is it?
BRUCE: I think so. Conference not giving you a hard time, is it?
MARY-ELLEN: Not at all. I'm only … I went to visit my friend.
BRUCE: Suzie?
MARY-ELLEN: No no, my sick friend. The journalist I was so excited to meet. Mark. I always speak of Mark.
BRUCE: Yeah?
MARY-ELLEN: He's much worse.
BRUCE: Oh well, that's no good.
MARY-ELLEN: I suppose I'm …
BRUCE: You feel sad for him and …
MARY-ELLEN: Yes.
BRUCE: Yeah. No good. Some mail here.
MARY-ELLEN: Oh.
BRUCE: I'll open it.
MARY-ELLEN: I was very happy with this thing here, the international marketing conference. Delegates paid three thousand dollars.
BRUCE: Whacko, hey.

MARY-ELLEN: I spoke about metrics in marketing.
BRUCE: Great. Really great.
MARY-ELLEN: Yeah.
BRUCE: A lot of bills coming in.
MARY-ELLEN: Bruce, I had hoped I could do something to help my friend Mark.
BRUCE: Like what?
MARY-ELLEN: Well, I don't think he particularly wants my help, so I'm feeling a bit …
BRUCE: He has his own family, Eme. Doesn't he?
MARY-ELLEN: Yes, but I had planned to …

Silence.

BRUCE: Have you dropped out?
MARY-ELLEN: No, I'm still here.
BRUCE: What is it you planned to do? I think you dropped out.
MARY-ELLEN: It doesn't matter. There's nothing I can do for him.
BRUCE: Oh well, Possum.
MARY-ELLEN: 'Possum'?
BRUCE: I'm trying to think of the Dame Edna thing about helping friends.
MARY-ELLEN: Will I love it?
BRUCE: Yes, but I've forgotten it [*the mail*]. Hang about. You got a letter from the House of Commons …
MARY-ELLEN: What is it, Bruce?
BRUCE: You've been called up for the Leveson Inquiry. Think you'd better come home, Eme.

SCENE THREE: NEWS 3

VIDEO: J.K. Rowling, David Cameron, Hugh Grant, Steve Coogan, Charlotte Church, Piers Morgan and others appear at the Leveson Inquiry.

SCENE FOUR: RESCUE ATTEMPTS

A big old telephone rings in Washington.
SURTITLE: *'Washington, British Foreign Office residence'*
An upper-class British man, JOHN COLVIN, *answers the telephone.*

ACT TWO 51

AMERICAN OPERATOR: This is a call for Mr Colvin.
JOHN: [*on the phone*] Thank you.
AMERICAN OPERATOR: The call is from Iran, sir.
JOHN: Go ahead, operator.
MARK: [*on the phone*] Dad!
JOHN: Hullo, Marco Polo. Are you alright?

> MARK *is back in Iran in 1979.*

MARK: No. I'm shit-scared.
JOHN: Why?
MARK: I think I might be going to die.
JOHN: Where are you?

> SURTITLE: *'Tehran, 1979'*

MARK: The Intercontinental. We're holed up here. Dad, I've seen them take to people with metal poles. My cameraman and I escaped a crowd. They turned on us. My translator is missing.
JOHN: It's the hostages crisis; is that what's shifted the mood?
MARK: It's been on the BBC and Iranian radio.
JOHN: Stay in the hotel. The mission failed disastrously.
MARK: Dad, if Carter sends in another raid to get the hostages they'll besiege this hotel. We're not safe, no one who looks remotely American. I need to know whether I stay or try to flee.
JOHN: Don't flee yet.
MARK: Do you think any of your 'political connections' might know about another U.S. mission?

> *Also on the line, elsewhere, are* IRANIAN OFFICERS *listening into the call and taking notes.*

You there? You didn't drop out, did you?
JOHN: I'm here, Mark. Can you stay by this phone line?
MARK: I'm not moving
JOHN: Buck up. Be back with you.

> MARK *puts down the telephone.* JOHN *goes. The phone rings.*

MARK: [*on his phone*] Hello …

> *The caller is* MARY-ELLEN—*in 2012.*

MARY-ELLEN: [*on her phone*] Mark?

MARK: Mary-Ellen?
MARY-ELLEN: Is this a weird time to call?
MARK: Oh well, a little.

1979 remains around him. The IRANIANS *are still eavesdropping.*

MARY-ELLEN: I've woken you up.
MARK: No no, you haven't.
MARY-ELLEN: Well, everything is relatively good with me. Some disasters, but I wanted to let you know about Leveson.
MARK: Oh.
MARY-ELLEN: I know. I'm attending the preliminary hearings at the Queen Elizabeth Buildings at Parliament. I thought you'd be interested. I'm to be a core participant. Ought to breathe new life into my court case too: a bit of public pressure on Elle.
MARK: Yes. No, that, that's very good.
MARY-ELLEN: I thought you'd want to cover it.
MARK: Not anymore. I can let the ABC Correspondent in London know to contact you.
MARY-ELLEN: But you said 'No' to my offer, Mark.
MARK: That's right.
MARY-ELLEN: It's the things I said about you, your childhood. About your father. It was insensitive of me.
MARK: Not entirely. Some of it was fair. You stirred up one or two things for me, Mary-Ellen.
MARY-ELLEN: I'm sorry if I did.

WILLIAM COLVIN *enters.*

MARK: I do have to go. Thank you.

MARY-ELLEN *vanishes.*

WILLIAM: Dad. Brought you the …

WILLIAM *has a charger for an iPad. Iran has gone. It is 2012. They are in Mark's room at the hospital in Sydney.*

MARK: Ahh, much appreciated, Will.
WILLIAM: So you're wrong about the 'Kony 2012' thing.
MARK: Oh yeah?
WILLIAM: [*Mark's iPad*] Ah nah shit. This isn't the … You have the old charger port. Must be Mum's.

ACT TWO

MARK: Really? I said my cord. You might have checked, shit, William.
WILLIAM: Not my fault. They changed it. Blame fuckin' Apple.
MARK: Well, yes, Steve-fucking Steve-fucking-Jobs.
WILLIAM: Yeah.
MARK: Tyrant. A complete fucking—
WILLIAM: Corpse.
MARK: [*with a laugh*] Still an arsehole.
WILLIAM: Bit shitty today?
MARK: No, I was much brighter today actually. I just wanted to sit and read and enjoy Twitter.
WILLIAM: I'll go home and—
MARK: No, you won't.
WILLIAM: It's cool.
MARK: It's not cool.
WILLIAM: So the new complications. What are they?
MARK: More of the same. Not something I'm particularly worried about.
WILLIAM: Right. Yeah, Kony's had forty million views since Monday.
MARK: Uploading a—frankly, rather shonky / documentary onto YouTube. /
WILLIAM: / I know that. / Vimeo. Vimeo is the platform for serious filmmakers.
MARK: Yes. Thank you. If you characterise this as a serious—
WILLIAM: No, I don't actually.
MARK: Maybe you find it compelling as a digital polemic—
WILLIAM: Didn't say that, but—
MARK: But as somebody who spent a fair bit of time in Uganda it strikes me as glib and simplistic. As for the revenue it will generate: *Cui bono?*
WILLIAM: I know.
MARK: Do you?
WILLIAM: What's that again?
MARK: 'Who benefits'?
WILLIAM: Yeah. Y'shitty with the doctors or—
MARK: I am not shitty. [*Reaching for his iPad*] Joseph Kony hasn't been in Uganda for six years.
WILLIAM: Still.
MARK: Still what?

WILLIAM: Motivating millions of people into action in a way we've never seen before. Get used to it.
MARK: Clicking a button is not the same as a counter culture.
WILLIAM: Yeah, baby boomers' mission accomplished. Time to just die.

MARK tries to laugh.

Why are you lying to me?
MARK: Lying to you?
WILLIAM: About the complications. What don't we know?
MARK: Well, they tell me the vessels from my leg implanted in my arm will be robust enough soon, y'know, for their mighty fuck-off needles.
WILLIAM: This is the fistula. I googled it so—
MARK: Far better than this horrid plug in my chest. And the cellulitis is resolving.
WILLIAM: Dad, I'm the only person on the planet—
MARK: Will. Come on.
WILLIAM: Well, aren't I? Aren't I?
MARK: William …

Mark's phone rings. He looks at the caller ID.

WILLIAM: Your specialist?
MARK: No. No, someone else.

He cancels the call.

WILLIAM: Nic and Mum aren't the same blood type and—take my fucking kidney.
MARK: I cannot countenance something so repugnant. Please.
WILLIAM: Why?
MARK: You are not to bring it up again.
WILLIAM: Why? Why?
MARK: Look, I didn't mean to be churlish about the iPad charger.
WILLIAM: And Kony.
MARK: It doesn't matter.
WILLIAM: Well, it does. Y'being a dick.
MARK: It's just without the iPad I sit here ruminating.

The IRANIANS reappear, listening in.

WILLIAM: Dad, you say you're not— Like, you say a father can't deprive a son of a spare kidney, but you're willing to, like …

ACT TWO

WILLIAM *stops before his voice chokes.*

MARK: Would you …? I can probably manage to get myself down to the cafe if you wanted to hang around for dinner.
WILLIAM: I'm going to see Nic's band play but.
MARK: Oh are you? Is that at the Metro?
WILLIAM: Oxford Art Factory.
MARK: That won't be until much later.
WILLIAM: I have to do things first.
MARK: I'd very much like to be there myself tonight. Tell your brother that.
WILLIAM: Yep. Next time dialysis fails you'll take— That's more fucked, much more fucked of you, to take away my dad.

WILLIAM *exits.*

JOHN: [*on the phone*] Polo?

Mark's father, JOHN, *has entered. The* IRANIANS *are listening.*

Son, I have spoken directly with people here in Washington—
MARK: What if they're listening—on the line?
JOHN: They may well be. Marco, with all certainty I can tell you the United States will not be sending in a second raid. The mood ought to temper. You'll be able to continue on doing your work.
MARK: Oh.
JOHN: Forgive me if I telegram your mother fibbing that you are making sensible plans to return to London soon.
MARK: Tell her I am safe. I will be now.
JOHN: Did the world of good to hear your voice again, I must say, Polo.
MARK: You too, Dad.
JOHN: You keep at it. Don't stop now. Go on and thrive, my boy.

JOHN *exits.*

MARY-ELLEN *appears in London.*

MARY-ELLEN: 'Will you think about my offer?

SURTITLE: *'Sent from Mary-Ellen Field's iPad on 12/06/2012 at 2:10 p.m. [excerpt]'*

'You wouldn't be taking anything you know. It's about giving and receiving, not taking.'

MARK: ' ... if you wanted to try it and see what happens, we could give it a go, but only (a) if you and Bruce are 100% agreed, (b) if your cardiologist really doesn't think it's a problem, and (c) you feel free to back out at any time. I am completely aware that it could fall over anyway at any time for medical/technical reasons, so please don't think I'll have hopes riding on it. I am so grateful that you would even have offered.
M.'

>SURTITLE: 'From: Mark Colvin Subject: Kidney Date: 17 June 2012 12:01:17 GMT+01: 00. To: Mary-Ellen Field [excerpt]'

SCENE FIVE: MORE NEPHROLOGY

Continued from Act One, Scene One.
PROFESSOR ZOLTAN ENDRE *sips his Coke Zero.*

ZOLTAN: Why do you want to do this? Just remind me again, would you?
MARY-ELLEN: I just know, apart from marrying my husband, having my children, it is the most important thing I'll ever do.
JUNIOR PHYSICIAN: In a spiritual sense?
MARY-ELLEN: I suppose.
ZOLTAN: A superstitious reason is kind of okay, depending on who you speak to. But, are there any other compelling reasons that we should know, that your family should know perhaps?
MARY-ELLEN: I don't know.
ZOLTAN: No?
MARY-ELLEN: No.
ZOLTAN: Or is it, it's like wanting to join the Yakuza in Japan. Cut off your finger to prove you're a courageous person.
MARY-ELLEN: I wouldn't say it like that.
SENIOR PHYSICIAN: Could you get out of this arrangement?
MARY-ELLEN: I don't want to. I am here entirely of my own volition.
ZOLTAN: Yep. You have to do something good for the world and this is what you've decided to do. Yep. Noble. Very. I still need to check you're not insane.
MARY-ELLEN: Dame Edna Everage's mother used to say there are no strangers, only friends you haven't met yet. Her mother is now in a maximum security twilight home. I think that's the joke.

ACT TWO

SENIOR PHYSICIAN: Is it?
JUNIOR PHYSICIAN: What?

They don't laugh.

MARY-ELLEN: I think.

ZOLTAN: Right. I'm more talking about a paranoid schizophrenic who's promised a kidney and promised someone else they'll buy them the Sydney Opera House. And I am concerned about the expectation from your side. Y'know: 'You've got to be my buddy now. I came in off the street and gave you my kidney so you have to come home and meet my mother.' That's not okay.

MARY-ELLEN: That won't happen. My mother's a terrible person.

ZOLTAN: So, just to get it out of the way, what you're asking us to do to you, the significant risk during surgery …

He holds a letter opener, a tribal looking dagger.

We can't always do laparoscopic, so could be back to the old days: do a loin incision.

He demonstrates on his own body with the dagger pointed at the rear of his abdomen.

Pretty big incision. There are three layers of muscle, each in different directions, right? Keeps all your stomach contents in.

He takes two random stapled pieces of paper from his desk. He levers them apart.

So you separate each of these layers out, right? You go in, you see the kidney sitting there.

He depicts the procedure with his hands.

Slowly peel around the kidney. Clamp the renal arteries close to the aorta. Close to the vena cava. Shell out the kidney. Sew it up. That's— that type of surgery, it's more than a tickle.

MARY-ELLEN: Alright.

ZOLTAN: Associated with several weeks in recovery. More surgical risk.

He picks up a biro to illustrate her ureter.

Damage to the ureter. Yeah, could happen. Other option is going through here …

He juts a hand into his tummy.

MARY-ELLEN: When someone else's life is at stake, worrying about scars is a bit ridiculous. At sixty-three it's not as if anyone is going to be looking at my tummy.

ZOLTAN: Bear with me. This way you've gotta push the bowel out of the way to get to the right plane. It's elaborate.

He takes the straw from his Coke Zero.

They put a tube in under the umbilicus.

Dark fluid drips on his papers and hands. He shakes it off.

They blow up the abdomen with some, ah, oxygen and a little CO_2. Plenty of room in there now to look around, and then through another port they thread in fibre optic instruments.

SENIOR PHYSICIAN: A camera.

ZOLTAN: Yeah, they use a camera. Tools go in through another port. We're visualising that on the screen. So. The guy's in there and he's directing and actually he's pushing a little bit hard there to get through the tissue and—whoops—

JUNIOR PHYSICIAN: Perforates your bowel.

ZOLTAN: Which is fine.

SENIOR PHYSICIAN: If he notices.

ZOLTAN: Minor perforations are promptly repaired. But he's looking through a very small aperture.

SENIOR PHYSICIAN: If he doesn't notice …

JUNIOR PHYSICIAN: You've got a bowel leak.

ZOLTAN: You end up at intensive care.

MARY-ELLEN: When can we do the tissue matching?

ZOLTAN: Sure. I need to be clear first up. You will suffer more than the recipient.

MARY-ELLEN: I think you've been pretty clear, yes.

ZOLTAN: He goes from feeling miserable, dialysed every few days, enduring years of chronic disease, to feeling terrific. You go from an intact healthy woman to an organ short.

MARY-ELLEN: Yes. That's fine. It's fine.

ZOLTAN sips his Coke Zero.

SENIOR PHYSICIAN: When's the second psychiatric review?

MARY-ELLEN: Another one?

ZOLTAN: To be scheduled.

MARY-ELLEN: I would like to see the report this time. I want a copy.
ZOLTAN: No, you don't need that. I'm also interested to judge the impact on your family, those who love you and—
MARY-ELLEN: That's for me to handle. They don't want to stand in the way of what I need to do; they never have.
ZOLTAN: Yeah, so look, my current opinion is that, even if we got the very unlikely tissue matching, and got ourselves clear of the psychiatric things, my current sense, and I want to be up-front, is that your other health factors will prohibit donation.
MARY-ELLEN: But that's not right. It's not fair.

> ZOLTAN *sips more Coke Zero, watching her. They are all watching her.*

I went to see my cardiologist and the syncope team at Royal Brompton in Chelsea. He held my hand and told me what a wonderful thing it was to do and they would do everything they could to help. He assured me that the pacemaker would not prevent me donating a kidney, so what are these other health issues?
JUNIOR PHYSICIAN: Cytomegalovirus?
ZOLTAN: Oh yeah, we'll soon know about that.
MARY-ELLEN: I would like to know what the alternative is. Your patient dies. Do you want that?
ZOLTAN: Mark Colvin is not my patient. You are.

SCENE SIX: BLOOD LETTING 3

MARK *is having dialysis whilst using his iPad.* MARY-ELLEN, *dishevelled, arrives with a drip stand.*

MARK: Mary-Ellen, what've they done to you?
MARY-ELLEN: I'm fine.
MARK: No, you're not. What's that?
MARY-ELLEN: [*the drip stand*] Nothing. Apparently I was a bit dehydrated. I bet my hair's a bird's nest, is it? They said I might faint so I had to lie down, which isn't very pleasant when you have to scoff a revolting old Monte Carlo. They couldn't find a vein so I've been stuck through like a complete druggie.
MARK: I'd give you my chair but I'm all rigged up.

There's a commode chair nearby.

MARY-ELLEN: This'll do.
MARK: No no, I think that's a toilet aid.
MARY-ELLEN: Not terribly elegant.

She sits on the commode chair.

MARK: You're sure you are alright?
MARY-ELLEN: Yes.
MARK: You're not.
MARY-ELLEN: No. Marko, the femoral angiogram ...
MARK: Is it bad?
MARY-ELLEN: I have a rare genetic condition.
MARK: Oh, dear.
MARY-ELLEN: 'Fibromuscular' something. It means nothing for *my* health, but ... I've failed you, Mark.
MARK: Mary-Ellen ...
MARY-ELLEN: Now they have their excuse because they think I'll spin out under the pressure or some utter rot.
MARK: I'm relieved.
MARY-ELLEN: Relieved? This is a disaster.
MARK: So I have to go back on the waiting list. Not my first jaunt down the River Styx. If you sacrificed a kidney and suffered for it I'd never forgive myself.
MARY-ELLEN: Stop it, I'm not listening. I'm giving you permission to be angry with me. I told you I could help.
MARK: You tried. I even hate seeing you like this now.
MARY-ELLEN: Be angry.
MARK: With what?
MARY-ELLEN: With this. With all of this.
MARK: Really? I think I've learnt to be a rather fatalistic person. I met victims of the Khmer Rouge. I covered famines in Ethiopia. I know I am fortunate.
MARY-ELLEN: No. You look me in the eyes. Mark. Look. Oh God, there's just no colour in them at all, Mark.
MARK: Thanks for that.
MARY-ELLEN: Sometimes positive thoughts, just believing—that can help.
MARK: And what, wish upon a star?
MARY-ELLEN: You think my blind faith is stupid, don't you?
MARK: No, I don't.

ACT TWO

MARY-ELLEN: The judge does. I keep promising Elle is going to testify. I can't say there's been a settlement. She denies it.

MARK: You're putting up with all that being stabbed and jabbed for my sake.

MARY-ELLEN: In here, with you, I have felt fantastically free. Finally something good was to come of it all, as though there's some purpose to everything I've been subjected to.

MARK: No, Mary-Ellen, that's not how it goes. You do know you were brilliant at Leveson, don't you? That counts.

MARY-ELLEN: I don't know what I'm clinging on for: some old bloke in a robe to proclaim in Her Maj's that the things they said about me were wrong. The costs are through the roof and I don't know what's going to happen. Justice is for the rich: mostly men who can afford the cleverest lawyers—and lawyers with no morals at all.

MARK: You don't believe that, Mary-Ellen.

MARY-ELLEN: Don't I? Women have only had legal rights for a century. Before that—merely chattels—owned by husbands and fathers and brothers and eventually even sons. I must have been mad to think I'd ever get justice.

ZOLTAN enters.

ZOLTAN: Hi. Do you mind if I speak to you together?

MARY-ELLEN: Go on. I know you all think I'm batshit crazy—

MARK: Mary-Ellen. Let him speak.

ZOLTAN: Your fibromuscular dysplasia is a concern, but we've agreed not insurmountable. You have the required negatives for the tissue and you have other things that match that are unusual. It's uncanny. I'd swear you two are siblings. The transplant can go ahead as soon as you are well enough, Mark.

MARY-ELLEN: Oh. Marko.

She kisses MARK *on either cheek.*

Sorry, did I—? God, I hope I didn't bump your needles.

MARK *shakes his head, can't speak.*

ZOLTAN: Got any questions for me?

MARY-ELLEN: Yes. When?

ZOLTAN: He's got to recover. Get a little stronger. A month or so.

MARY-ELLEN: Mark, you're not saying anything.

MARK: Wow.

ZOLTAN: I'll also tell you, unequivocally, Mary-Ellen, that you are not and never were an alcoholic.

MARY-ELLEN: You...

ZOLTAN: Otherwise we'd be disqualifying you as a donor.

MARY-ELLEN: Oh, I ... might need some fresh air. I think I, um, might—I think I need a drink.

ZOLTAN: My shout. Doctor's orders. You've been too good.

MARK: I'd like to call my mother.

MARY-ELLEN: Oh do, yes, do, Mark. Can I say hello too?

MARK: No.

MARY-ELLEN: No. Lovely. Of course.

ZOLTAN: Mary-Ellen, do you think Bruce has managed Skype yet?

MARY-ELLEN: Probably not.

ZOLTAN: Okay. Only by this stage I would normally have had constant enquiries from a spouse.

MARY-ELLEN: I suppose I should, ah ...

ZOLTAN: I mean obviously your family trust you, which is great, but now it's a reality so ...

MARY-ELLEN: There's that and, well, I'm still yet to tell Bruce.

MARK: You have told Bruce.

MARY-ELLEN: No no, I haven't, actually.

ZOLTAN: But you didn't— Did you lie to us?

MARY-ELLEN: Not really. No. Never.

ZOLTAN: That's despicable. How could you do such a thing to your husband?

MARY-ELLEN: Excuse me? I think I know my husband.

ZOLTAN: What about your marriage?

MARY-ELLEN: What about yours? You've had a few.

ZOLTAN: How do you know that?

MARK: I'm sorry, I may have told Mary-Ellen that, Zoltan.

ZOLTAN: Did you? Right.

MARY-ELLEN: So don't either of you two get on your high horses about my marriage.

MARK: Mary-Ellen, it's not happening—not unless Bruce approves.

SCENE SEVEN: LINGUINE

MARY-ELLEN *watches* BRUCE *eat his linguine. The restaurant is busy.*

MARY-ELLEN: How is it, the linguine?
BRUCE: You know it's my favourite.

MARY-ELLEN *shifts the cheese from her salad.*

MARY-ELLEN: I asked for no cheese.
BRUCE: No cheese. Not drinking. Anyone'd think you're pregnant.
MARY-ELLEN: [*through a laugh*] Because I'm normally such an alcoholic?
BRUCE: [*eating*] No.
MARY-ELLEN: I'm feeling fit.
BRUCE: You're—mouth full, pardon me—you look wonderful, you always do.

She pinches some food from his plate.

MARY-ELLEN: 'All you see is pasta.' I mean … 'Everything you see I owe to pasta.'
BRUCE: Who's that?
MARY-ELLEN: Probably buggering up the quote.
BRUCE: Is it Sophia Loren?
MARY-ELLEN: Yes, I was quoting her.
BRUCE: Is she dead?
MARY-ELLEN: No.

BRUCE *has his mobile phone.*

BRUCE: Something tells me she is.

BRUCE *puts on his reading glasses.*

MARY-ELLEN: Darling, we're not going to check it now. We're at dinner.

Silence. He searches for the answer on his phone.

Goodness, Brucie. How did we ever get by before all this?
BRUCE: Hang on a sec.
MARY-ELLEN: Wikipedia, darling, Wikipedia.

BRUCE *scrolls on his phone. Silence.*

You know my friend Mark …
BRUCE: Dead. It says she's dead.

MARY-ELLEN: Really? Sophia Loren? That can't be right. Surely I would have known.

BRUCE: A loss.

He screen-locks his phone. Silence. She watches him eat.

My doctor's not too happy.

MARY-ELLEN: What? Why?

BRUCE: More scans he reckons, but I'm—it's um—it looks like it could be a visit to the cardiologist again soon.

MARY-ELLEN: What can we do?

BRUCE: Cull the stress. Everything I'm already doing. Glad you're back.

MARY-ELLEN: Bruce … my friend Mark …

BRUCE: How is he?

MARY-ELLEN: I want to give him one of my kidneys.

BRUCE: Oh, yeah? Pull the other one.

MARY-ELLEN: My left kidney.

BRUCE: What?

MARY-ELLEN: I've investigated this and, well, I am, I'm going to give Mark Colvin my spare kidney and it'll save his life.

BRUCE: You are going to do fucking what?

Other DINERS *have heard.*

MARY-ELLEN: Now listen. In Australia, as well as working, I've been having tests to match tissues samples and blood. And I match. I'm a better match than anyone else on the planet.

BRUCE: You've actually—you've bloody promised this to him? You can't—

MARY-ELLEN: Now, you're entitled to be cross—

BRUCE: Wait—

MARY-ELLEN: I want you to know—

BRUCE: Now hang on—

MARY-ELLEN: Just—chill. I want you to know something.

BRUCE: What? No, I want to talk.

MARY-ELLEN: Yes, I was being bossy. You talk.

BRUCE: Well, no, I don't have anything to say, but— No. I am saying 'no'. You can't. And, and, even if I did let you, your doctors won't allow it.

MARY-ELLEN: They've absolutely cleared this. I'm scheduled for the surgery. I've had to pee in buckets and give gallons of blood and do an angiogram. They shoot a dye all through you and—

ACT TWO

BRUCE: And you've been through these procedures and and and—without me?

MARY-ELLEN: I'm a big girl. I gave birth twice.

BRUCE: And wasn't I there for that? You can't do this; you're a mother.

MARY-ELLEN: The boys don't have the same blood group as me, so even if a catastrophe happened they can't have my kidney and nor can you.

BRUCE: You're a mother. It's not just about you. You're needed.

MARY-ELLEN: Bruce, Justin and Tim are over thirty, all grown up, and I don't even cross the road unless the little man goes red—I mean green—goes green. Ha, almost got hit by a bus then, didn't I? But no, and why shouldn't I do something that is …?

BRUCE: I can't believe you. You're sounding like a real fruit cake.

Silence. A WAITRESS *arrives at their side.*

WAITRESS: Everything good?

MARY-ELLEN: Yes thank you.

WAITRESS: All good?

MARY-ELLEN: Lovely.

BRUCE: Thank you.

WAITRESS: Some more water here?

MARY-ELLEN: No, thank you. Thank you.

WAITRESS: Alright. Good then. Enjoy your meal.

MARY-ELLEN *retrieves an envelope and gently unfolds a letter.*

MARY-ELLEN: I'd like you to read this little bit of paper I have. It is from Professor Zoltan Endre, Director of Nephrology at Prince of Wales Hospital, Randwick. It's all here, Bruce. It states that I am a sane, rational person. I am not, and never was, an addict. Things people said against me were untrue.

BRUCE: Good. You've got your Merit Certificate. Now call this stunt off.

MARY-ELLEN *retracts the letter. She carefully folds it again. He beckons her to hand it over. She resists.*

MARY-ELLEN: It is my body, Bruce. It's mine.

BRUCE: And this is my—our—marriage, and you kept me out of this. You deceived me. I have to—I think we should go.

MARY-ELLEN: No, no.

BRUCE: I want to see Tim. The boys don't know—do they …?

MARY-ELLEN: No-one knows.

BRUCE: This man knows. All these doctors know.

MARY-ELLEN: There was no sense worrying you until I knew I could and that Mark would accept my offer. He resisted, even though he is at death's door. And he'll only do it now—only if you say yes.

BRUCE: A journalist, a fucking journalist. He just wants the story.

MARY-ELLEN: He stopped reporting my case as soon as I proposed this. I knew he would so I kept it to myself while I did my research. I had two men to manage so it was better to keep you both in the dark. I didn't want you to try to stop me.

BRUCE: That's the real reason. That's it. Of course I'd stop you.

MARY-ELLEN: I also knew if you'd said 'No', I would have had to disobey you, which I would not have wanted to do, but would have done because I know that we have a wonderful forty-year marriage. We have brought up two beautiful sons together. It hasn't always been easy but our union has always been the surest thing and I was sure it could stand this deception. I'm determined, I am determined to do it. Darling … He's really sick, darling.

BRUCE: I don't care about him. It's you I'm worried about. I don't know this fucking man you met on the internet.

MARY-ELLEN: Well, when you say it like that.

BRUCE: It's the fucking truth! I don't want to hear about him. You're making this my choice whether he lives or dies. I don't want it put to me like that, Mary-Ellen. It's you I am married to. It's you I love. You.

People are aware of their argument.

I'll get the bill. Grab your coat.

MARY-ELLEN: You're eating your linguine.

BRUCE: No. I hate it. I hate the taste now. It's ruined.

He flings his fork into the sauce with a splash of red.

MARY-ELLEN: Alright, honey. Maybe I shouldn't have done this here.

BRUCE: Oh, because do you think it's a bit manipulative?

BRUCE *mops up the spill.*

Fuck.

MARY-ELLEN: He has septicaemia again, Bruce. The real risk is he is becoming resistant to antibiotics.

ACT TWO

BRUCE has a stain on his clothes.

BRUCE: Look. Fuck.
MARY-ELLEN: He has two sons. They must be so frightened.

She puts her napkin in water and hands it to him. Silence.

BRUCE: I, ah, I don't want to speak to—I never want to meet him. If you do it, you come back and you're never allowed to contact him again.
MARY-ELLEN: If you think that is necessary.
BRUCE: I do. I think it is necessary for us. And and and it would have to be anonymous.
MARY-ELLEN: I've already decided that.
BRUCE: No-one could ever know. Not even our friends. Ever. I don't want some smart bastard at the golf club saying to me, 'Oh this man, does he think about your wife every time he has a piss?'
MARY-ELLEN: That is—
BRUCE: Well, I don't know.
MARY-ELLEN: —hilarious.
BRUCE: Well, I'm not trying to be funny, am I? And I'm not saying I accept this.
MARY-ELLEN: I agree: anonymous.
BRUCE: This family has had enough—
MARY-ELLEN: Absolutely. No more intrusions.
BRUCE: You lay down the law with him because a journalist might, y'know ... they're media. They're publicity sluts.
MARY-ELLEN: Not this one.
BRUCE: I reckon there's a pretty healthy dose of narcissism—a job like his, fronting a radio program and …
MARY-ELLEN: No-one will ever know about this. Ironclad.
BRUCE: Don't do it, Mary-Ellen. It will not make life better.

SURTITLE: 'Sophia Loren is alive. Her death was an internet hoax.'

The WAITRESS *approaches.*

WAITRESS: Hello, Mary-Ellen.
MARY-ELLEN: Yes?
WAITRESS: I'm your anaesthetist today.
MARY-ELLEN: Oh. Alright.

WAITRESS: I'm Dr Stavrakis. Would you like to lie on the table?
MARY-ELLEN: Thank you.
WAITRESS: If I can explain, I've been having a bit of trouble finding a vein.
MARY-ELLEN: Yes, they always do with me.
WAITRESS: I see. So what I would like to do is inject into your neck.
MARY-ELLEN: Oh, is that a thing, is it?
WAITRESS: Not the best for you, I'm afraid. I've put some numbing cream on there, but you will feel a stick.

She injects MARY-ELLEN*'s neck.*

MARY-ELLEN: Oh. Oh, yes.
WAITRESS: Bit of a stick going in. Not too much longer. Now if you can keep talking.
MARY-ELLEN: Yes.
WAITRESS: How was your day?
MARY-ELLEN: Pardon?
WAITRESS: You can talk about anything you like.
MARY-ELLEN: Ah…
WAITRESS: How was your day? Nice, was it, Mary-Ellen?
MARY-ELLEN: Um…
WAITRESS: Yep.
MARY-ELLEN: Was…
WAITRESS: Ah-ha.
MARY-ELLEN: I played…
WAITRESS: Okay.
MARY-ELLEN: iPhone played … 'How Sweet … It Is'.
BRUCE: 'This is your big week darling for you and Mark .I am praying for you and just wish I could be at your side.God is watching over you.for Ever my love
XXXX
Bruce'

   SURTITLE: *'Email from Bruce Westwood 16 March 2013 at 15:54:41 GMT'*

   BRUCE *exits.*

MARY-ELLEN: The sun was—James Taylor and … I was believing. I kept believing …

SCENE EIGHT: INSIDE ORGANS

MARY-ELLEN *is turned over. In surgery, with glimpses of blood and fat reminiscent of pasta sauce ...*

Voices becomes audible to a sedated MARY-ELLEN.

RUPERT MURDOCH: *'I don't know, you know in my heart, I'm not going to ask you now, but I would have thought a hundred percent—but at least ninety per cent—of payments were made at the instigation of cops, saying, "I've got a good story here. It's worth five hundred quid", or something. And you would say, "No, it's not", or "We'll check it out", or whatever. And they'd say, "Well, we'll ring the* Mirror *..."* [Whispering] *It was the culture of Fleet Street.'*

> SURTITLE: *'March 6, 2013. Thomas More Square, East London. Rupert Murdoch is secretly recorded by a Sun journalist in the newspaper's headquarters. [Text abridged, first published by Xaro]'*

'I remember when I first bought the News of the World, *the first day I went to the office ... and there was a big wall safe ... And I said, "What's that for?" And they said, "We keep some cash in there". And I said, "What for?" They said, "Well, sometimes the editor needs some on a Saturday night for powerful friends. And sometimes the chairman is doing badly at the tables ..."'*

> *Laughter.*

'"... and he helps himself ..."'

> MARK *is being operated on at the same time.*

SUN STAFFER: *'Would it surprise you to know ... the first time I heard about the 1906 Misconduct Act was when I was arrested. No-one had ever told me about this in this company—'*

RUPERT MURDOCH: *'The first time I heard about it was a couple of weeks ago, but go on.'*

SUN STAFFER: *'You've got a police force desperate to make up for previous mistakes. [Our Management and Standards Committee] continue to hand over information on each and every person in this room—'*

RUPERT MURDOCH: *'No, they're not. No, they're not. Haven't given them anything for months.'*

SUN DEPUTY EDITOR: 'It would be nice to hit back when we can.'
RUPERT MURDOCH: 'We will, we will ... I've got to be careful what comes out—but frankly, I won't say it, but just trust me. Okay?'

SCENE NINE 'RECOVERY'

ZOLTAN: Mary-Ellen?

>MARY-ELLEN *computes her surrounds.* ZOLTAN *is with her.*

Would you like to see a photo of your kidney inside Mark?

>*She looks through him. He shows her his phone.*

You're a bit groggy. Can you see it there? One of the team took this pic. It really wanted to attach itself as soon as they removed the clamps. She's going like a train.

MARY-ELLEN: How ... how's ... Mark?

ZOLTAN: Mark is doing well.

MARY-ELLEN: Can I ...?

ZOLTAN: You can't see him yet; we've got you in isolation to guard against infection. I wanted you to know, though, it's all good. We did it in time. And it wasn't—it wasn't appropriate to say this until now but ... we did estimate Mark only had days.

MARY-ELLEN: Until?

ZOLTAN: Death. He's going to be alright. You've saved his life. So, good for you to know that. And now we've got to make sure we don't endanger yours. I have to get you up and moving. It's going to be uncomfortable, you're in pain, but it's important you are mobile today. If the pain is too much there's a button here. You press it.

>MARY-ELLEN *reaches for the button.*

Do you need it now? I can; I'll press it for you. Okay. It's okay.

>MARK *is in his hospital room.*

MARY-ELLEN: 'The surgeon said you are producing lots of pee, which is very good.'

>SURTITLE: *'Actual text messages sent 2in hospital 2nd-23rd March 2013'*

MARK: 'I'm pretty knocked around but v happy about my new kidney. Someone has started a new Twitter account called @colvinskidney'

MARY-ELLEN: 'Have you seen the photo your doc took of my kidney inside you?'
MARK: 'No.'
MARY-ELLEN: 'Here you go …'

    PROJECTION: *Mary-Ellen Field's kidney inside Mark Colvin.*

MARK: 'Wow.'
MARY-ELLEN: '… it was taken immediately after it started working, just the shade of pink they want. I told you I was giving you a perfect one.'
MARK: 'Two more patients going down for transplant today. One deceased donor. Good news for two families while one grieves.'
MARY-ELLEN: 'I've just had an enema, I hear you look great.'
MARK: 'Not sure about that, but they're going to let me have a shower.'
MARY-ELLEN: 'Just saw your previous message. Yes, it's terribly sad, but there's no tragedy in ours, only happiness …'

    SURTITLE: *'Tweet: '@colvinius @maryellenfield you are unaware of the facts. The truth'.*
    —@ellemacpherson 6 May 2013
    Tweet: 'So testify'—@Colvinius 6 May 2013'

SCENE TEN 'DEPARTURE'

MARK *is in his hospital room.* MARY-ELLEN *bounds in. She is dressed to depart.*

MARY-ELLEN: Mark. My God. Have you seen the article about you in today's paper?
MARK: Yeah. Why?
MARY-ELLEN: They mention my gender. They know. It means they know who I am.
MARK: I don't think it's any worry.
MARY-ELLEN: We went to such trouble, putting me on the other side of the hospital under another name. They've hacked my phone.
MARK: They wouldn't hack you here.
MARY-ELLEN: Of course they can—can do it from anywhere—offshore—the Maldives and these places. Nigeria. News is going to break the story.
MARK: I know people at News, trustworthy people. There's no evidence of hacking in Aus.

MARY-ELLEN: I don't trust them. I get to be in control. Not them. If there's one thing you've taught me—
MARK: You're entitled to do it how you please. Do you want to go public?
MARY-ELLEN: No. Bruce and I always said the donation is strictly a private matter.
MARK: I think you'd come off looking pretty good actually.
MARY-ELLEN: Are you insane? They'd say I did the whole thing for PR or something. I'm sorry, I probably sound ridiculous to you, Mark.
MARK: No.
MARY-ELLEN: But the friends I have made in the police tell me I need to be paranoid. I mean, at my last meeting with the Met, the senior detective realised we were being watched.
MARK: You didn't tell me this.
MARY-ELLEN: I didn't.
MARK: Why not?
MARY-ELLEN: You were sick. Worry isn't good. I know you do worry about me.

Silence.

MARK: So they've discharged you?
MARY-ELLEN: Hurrying me out the door now?
MARK: Honestly, I'm not.
MARY-ELLEN: I've had days to recover and it's routine surgery for them. I'm allowed to get back to work.
MARK: Great. Me too soon.
MARY-ELLEN: You get back there and hold sneaky politicians to account. That's all the thanks I want.

Silence.

The police are taking my case very seriously now. They've examined all the CCTV footage near where I live. It's a stalking investigation. Me. With stalkers. I bet most people would have it the other way around.
MARK: Extraordinary.
MARY-ELLEN: The way these nasty people operate. Maybe Bruce and I should go public. Know any decent journos?
MARK: Still a few kicking around. I'll put in a word.
MARY-ELLEN: I refused to sell my silence when they tried to buy it. I'm to

ACT TWO 73

be punished for that. They're taking a charge out on my house. News owns half my home.

MARK: How can they do that?

MARY-ELLEN: Because they defeated me. I was forced to withdraw. It means when Bruce and I die, our sons—especially Justin who needs care—will have a substantial chunk taken from their inheritance to pay for Rupert's London silks. People claim things changed at Leveson and the Senate Select Committees. They didn't. Rupert won.

MARK: You must tell me these things.

MARY-ELLEN: That goes for you too, Marko. When you can't sleep at night, it's my daytime.

MARK: Keep fighting your case, Mary-Ellen. Somehow.

MARY-ELLEN: Marko, when I walk past my mantelpiece, I'm not going to see Rupert's turkey jowls smiling in half the family photos. It's not over yet. Nor is it for you.

Silence.

Well, there'll be taxis at the taxi rank.

MARK: Yes, no need to call, I don't think. Be taxis.

MARY-ELLEN: Good. Yes. Well then …

MARK: Alright …

MARY-ELLEN: I'll toddle off.

MARK: We'll email. We'll text.

MARY-ELLEN: And Twitter. I'm addicted.

MARK: Good.

Silence.

MARY-ELLEN: I have another six weeks before I fly. That's my last check-up. You needn't worry about me pestering you. Do lay off junk food though, because I'll know; I feel it in your waters.

MARK: I have a hankering for Chiko Rolls.

MARY-ELLEN: How gross.

MARK: Yes.

Silence.

MARY-ELLEN: Marko, will you give a gigantic hug to your family from me?

MARK: Yeah … And Tim and Justin. And to Bruce. Say from me that I am most …

Silence.

MARY-ELLEN: Alright, well …

MARK lumbers towards her.

Alright, Mark?

He wraps his arms around her. He is crying.

There there, Marko. It's alright.

MARK: Thank you. Thank you.

They are hugging.

THE END

Belvoir presents

MARK COLVIN'S KIDNEY

By **TOMMY MURPHY**
Director **DAVID BERTHOLD**

This production of Mark Colvin's Kidney *opened at Belvoir St Theatre on Wednesday 1 March 2017.*

Set Designer **MICHAEL HANKIN**
Costume Designer **JULIE LYNCH**
Lighting Designer **DAMIEN COOPER**
Composer & Sound Designer **NATE EDMONDSON**
Projection Design **VEXRAN PRODUCTIONS**
Movement Director **SCOTT WITT**
Directorial Secondment **HUGO KOEHNE**
Stage Manager **LUKE McGETTIGAN**
Assistant Stage Manager **KEIREN SMITH**
Stage Management Secondment **DANA SPENCE**
Production Manager **SALLY WITHNELL**
Assistant Production Manager **AMANDA CAPUTI**

With

PETER CARROLL
KIT ESURUOSO
JOHN HOWARD
SARAH PEIRSE
CHRISTOPHER STOLLERY
HELEN THOMSON

Mark Colvin's Kidney was co-commissioned with Playwriting Australia.

Mark Colvin's Kidney has been supported by Macquarie Group employees and the Macquarie Group Foundation under its staff support policy.

Sarah Peirse

PRODUCTION THANKS
Audio Visual Events

PHOTOGRAPHY
Brett Boardman

DESIGN
Alphabet Studio

WRITER'S NOTE
Tommy Murphy

This is the play in which renal defeats venal. We can thank actor, John Howard, for coining that phrase. In our final script workshop, Sarah Peirse, who plays Mary-Ellen Field, noted a turning point. Her character concludes that the structures she trusted – the law, the state, the press, even the simple decency of her fellow humans – have failed her. The turning point comes with the choice she makes. In an ethically deficient world, the individual can only take charge of one person's actions – her own. In identifying this, I heard Sarah explain to me the heart of the story.

Many people contribute to the making of a play. For this one in particular that includes some real living people. Those I managed to reach granted me their trust and wisdom. I thank them.

Belvoir's Artistic Director, Eamon Flack, provided the initial provocation that triggered the hunt for '...a play that is local and global'. I had already been curious about creating a journalist character. The forces of change on the profession and a journalist's daily wrestle with matters of principle seemed delicious for drama. I suggested to Eamon that a play centring on a foreign correspondent might fit the bill. Seeking inspiration, I spoke to many journos both abroad and locally – one who lived across the road in fact. They all offered glimpses into brilliant lives and striking moments of ethical quandary. I even began a draft about one bright spark. He'd got himself into a pickle in the United States and was arrested for doing his job. Great. Several scenes into my draft he apparently hired a clever lawyer and got away with it. Good for him. But my second act vanished.

He is on notice to continue to live a life rich with dramatic incident and get back to me. Along the way he suggested I speak to his mentor, a person who is a guiding figure for many...

I shadowed Mark Colvin at ABC radio for an afternoon as he made his flagship national current affairs program *PM*. Here it was. He was describing scenes. Did he see my eyes light up at the exchanges of dialogue I was desperate to scribble down there and then?

I was a stranger and he had begun the first draft of *Light and Shadow: Memoirs of a Spy's Son*. He could very well have told me to go and get stuffed. However, like all the journalists I met, Mark had been on the other side of an obfuscating interviewee. He displayed a professional duty to share the truth. And he did not stand in the way of someone who was keen to file a story. So he permitted me to go right ahead. What a guy!

The mode of making the play began to echo its content: interviews, recorded voice, and the way distance can achieve an intimate connection. Mark arranged for me to meet Mary-Ellen Field via Skype. I have the recordings, with permission. I began with, 'So tell me, how did this go from a tweet to an organ donation?' I heard her wonderful laugh for the first time.

Mark would call me on long car trips. I'd conduct an interview, sometimes nervously as he is one of the great interviewers in the country. I tried to apply his own advice. 'Why?' is often the best question. Listening is the most important thing. I'd get lost in his stories, lost with that voice, and have to remind myself to respond because this time he was not on my kitchen radio.

Tommy Murphy

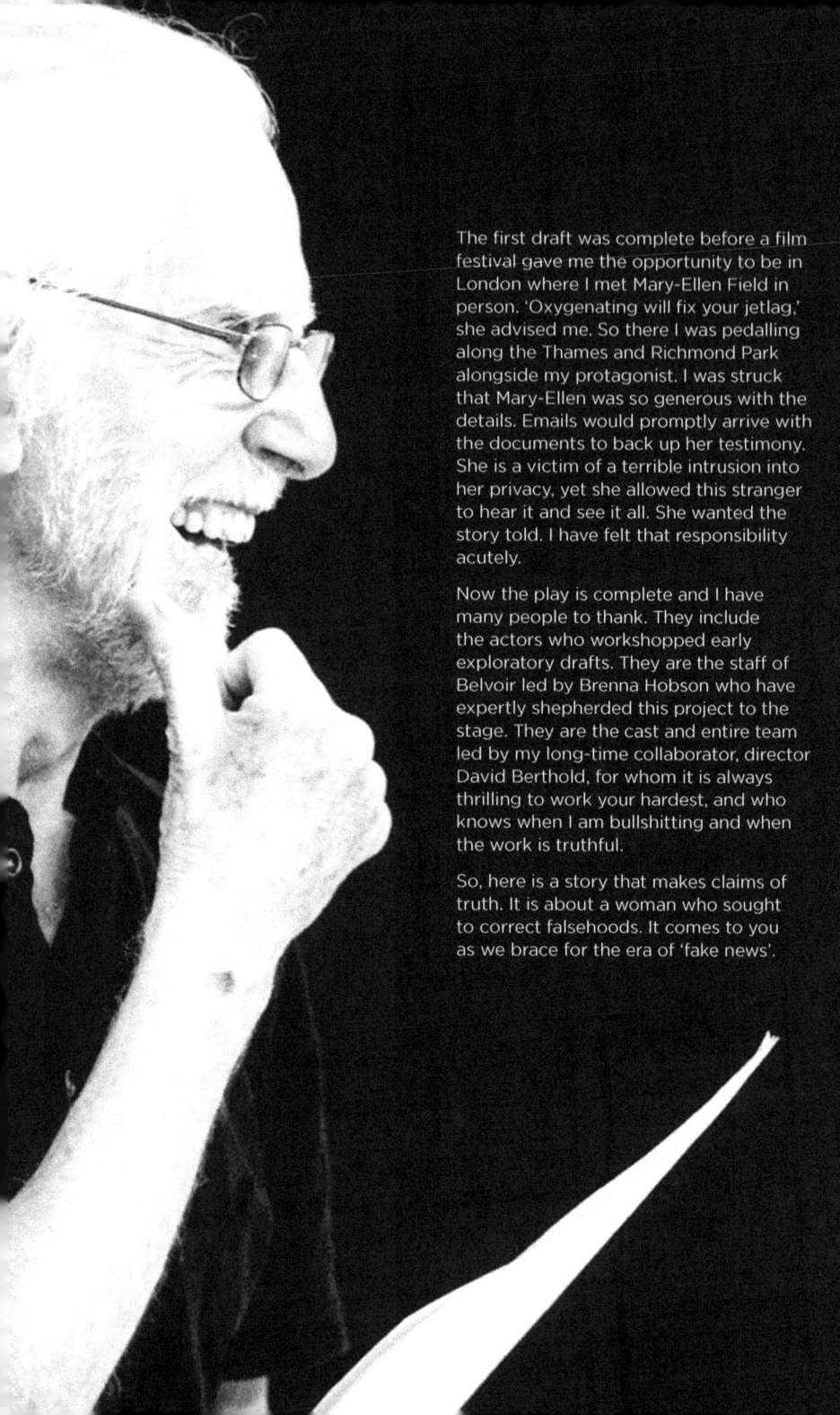

The first draft was complete before a film festival gave me the opportunity to be in London where I met Mary-Ellen Field in person. 'Oxygenating will fix your jetlag,' she advised me. So there I was pedalling along the Thames and Richmond Park alongside my protagonist. I was struck that Mary-Ellen was so generous with the details. Emails would promptly arrive with the documents to back up her testimony. She is a victim of a terrible intrusion into her privacy, yet she allowed this stranger to hear it and see it all. She wanted the story told. I have felt that responsibility acutely.

Now the play is complete and I have many people to thank. They include the actors who workshopped early exploratory drafts. They are the staff of Belvoir led by Brenna Hobson who have expertly shepherded this project to the stage. They are the cast and entire team led by my long-time collaborator, director David Berthold, for whom it is always thrilling to work your hardest, and who knows when I am bullshitting and when the work is truthful.

So, here is a story that makes claims of truth. It is about a woman who sought to correct falsehoods. It comes to you as we brace for the era of 'fake news'.

Playwright's Thanks

Mark Colvin, Mary-Ellen Field, Bruce Westwood, William Colvin, Nicholas McKenzie, Michele McKenzie, Professor Zoltan Endre and the Prince of Wales Department of Nephrology, Playwriting Australia, The ABC archives, The Cameron Creswell Agency, Cait MacMahon and the DART Centre for Journalism and Trauma, Dr. Andrea Phelps, Yasmin Parry ABC digital producer, Emma Burnett, Jude Bunting, Chris Tange, James Hanning, James Baker, Michael Carey, Mick Fanning, Catherine Clare, Lucy Wirth, Anthony Blair, Needeya Islam, Hugh O'Keefe, Timothy 'Lady Di' Spencer, Angela Bowne, Raena Lea-Shannon, Baker & McKenzie Lawyers and Patricia and Philip Murphy and their brood.

The journos: James West, Sally Sara, Ali Benton, Suzie Smith, Sophie McNeill, Greg Wilesmith, Marianne Leitch, Jo Chichester, Mark Davis, Janine Cohen, Lucy McNally, Sally Virgoe, Scott Spark, Stephen Long, Sarah MacDonald, Simon Marnie, Toby Creswell and Jo Jarvis.

The actors who workshopped the script: Annie Byron, Thuso Lekapwe, Eryn Jean Norvill, William Zappa, Sacha Horler, Duncan Ragg, Callan Colley and the current cast.

And the beautiful Dane Crawford.

Peter Carroll and Sarah Peirse

DIRECTOR'S NOTE
David Berthold

Ripples of Hope

I remember being glued to the Leveson Inquiry. All that rigorous interrogation and the testimonies of the famous, including a fragile-looking Rupert Murdoch. It felt like we were witnessing the fall of a media empire. It felt like the world was about to change and that 'truth' and 'ethics' and 'justice' would somehow flourish.

Five years on, that feeling is foreign. 'Alternative facts' fight with the truth, and justice for many seems more distant than ever.

I was not aware of Mary-Ellen Field's story until Tommy Murphy, that most intrepid of playwrights, brought it to my attention. Things struck me with immediate force. Here was a very successful woman, a member of the Conservative Party, who bit by bit had her natural faith in the cornerstones of British justice eroded. More specifically, here was someone who had been treated savagely by the media and yet decided to give her kidney to a journalist. How does that happen?

Altruism is mysterious. Evolutionary biology and neurobiology tell us that we're hardwired for it, but that the trigger can be untouched. We are often suspicious of those who say they expect no reward for their kindness. The idea of absolute selflessness (is there such a thing?) doesn't quite gel in times when empathy seems to be in such short supply.

But, it happened. Mary-Ellen gave Mark a kidney, that spectacular centre of the body's waste disposal system. That act of kindness, in its private, personal way, helped to cleanse. It added, in its modest way, to the sum of goodness in the world. Perhaps, in the face of crushing malice and injustice, that is the best we can hope for. Perhaps, though, such acts, however small, accumulate and cultivate.

Perhaps *Mark Colvin's Kidney* can be part of that current, its own ripple of hope.

"Few will have the greatness to bend history itself, but each of us can work to change a small portion of events, and in the total of all those acts will be written the history of this generation. It is from numberless diverse acts of courage and belief that human history is shaped. Each time a man stands up for an ideal, or acts to improve the lot of others, or strikes out against injustice, he sends forth a tiny ripple of hope, and crossing each other from a million different centers of energy and daring, those ripples build a current that can sweep down the mightiest walls of oppression and resistance."

(Robert F. Kennedy, Day of Affirmation address delivered at the University of Capetown, South Africa, June 6, 1966)

David Berthold

SALLY SARA
Africa Correspondent, Australian Broadcasting Corporation.

We watched the clock intently on the day of Mark Colvin's kidney transplant. Not to keep to our newsroom deadlines, but wondering, just wondering if he was alright. Had they finished? Was it a success? Would it change his life?

Early in the day a Twitter account cheekily named @ColvinsKidney made its debut. Given Mark's prolific Twitter presence, it was only appropriate that his new kidney was getting in some practice. 'It's got his sense of humour,' we said, as if it were his offspring.

There were some tears that day. We were half worried, half hopeful. Most of us knew nothing of the donor or her story. It was a mystery. We didn't really want to know – it didn't matter. The main thing was that Mark had a lifesaving chance, a chance to improve the quality of his life.

Mark kept most of his medical battles to himself, but we had seen his condition worsening over many months. He lumbered to his desk with his walking stick, sometimes exhausted.

'You're a one man teaching hospital,' I said to Mark one afternoon. He laughed. He had endured more medication, surgery, complications and chronic pain than most could manage in a lifetime. His career as a foreign correspondent had been cut short by the chronic illness he contracted in Africa. But, he found other ways to engage with the world.

Mark was one of the first journalists in the country to fully harness the potential of Twitter. It was a way for him to communicate and collate. And he was bloody good at it. He was tweeting long before hipster blokes half his age had even sprouted their first chin hair.

Radio too, was a perfect medium for Mark. He could speak with people around the world in places his tired body would not allow him to visit.

At 5pm, when the theme sounded for ABC Radio's *PM* program, there was his voice. Audio honey. That's how I would describe it – rich and smooth. He could read aloud all the instructions to my white goods and I would listen intently.

His voice gave some clues to his background – the English accent, the fierce general knowledge and giant intellect. But, his most powerful sound of all, has always been silence. The uncomfortable silence of waiting on a politician who is avoiding a question or the generous silence when someone is struggling to explain a trauma or a truth.

Mark listens. Intently. On air and off. That listening brings trust and connection. He listened carefully, the first time Mary-Ellen Field spoke with him about her experience as a victim of the phone hacking scandal in the UK. It was the beginning of an unexpected friendship that would change both their lives – the product of the changing relationship between journalists and those we interview.

Years ago, journalists researched interviewees, not the other way around. But, now thanks to social media and search engines, we also leave our own detailed digital footprint. Our stories, our controversies and some of our personal details are only a few clicks away. Interviewees can check us out, before we check them out.

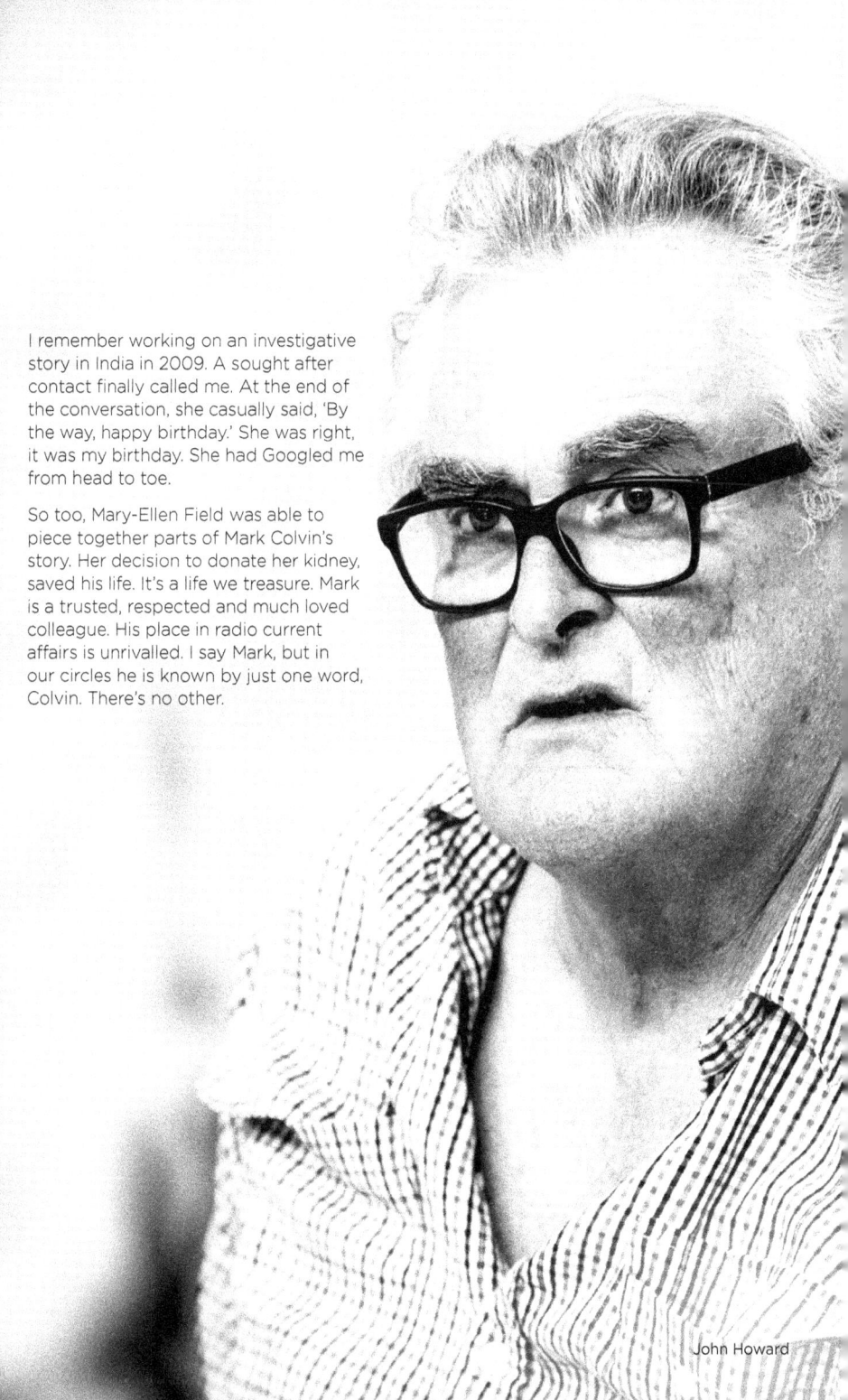

I remember working on an investigative story in India in 2009. A sought after contact finally called me. At the end of the conversation, she casually said, 'By the way, happy birthday.' She was right, it was my birthday. She had Googled me from head to toe.

So too, Mary-Ellen Field was able to piece together parts of Mark Colvin's story. Her decision to donate her kidney, saved his life. It's a life we treasure. Mark is a trusted, respected and much loved colleague. His place in radio current affairs is unrivalled. I say Mark, but in our circles he is known by just one word, Colvin. There's no other.

John Howard

BIOGRAPHIES

TOMMY MURPHY Writer

Tommy is an award-winning playwright and screenwriter. He is currently the Patrick White Fellow at Sydney Theatre Company. *Holding the Man*, Tommy's stage adaptation, continues to be produced across the world with upcoming productions in France, USA and Israel. His screenplay for *Holding the Man*, for which he was Associate Producer, won the Australian Writers' Guild Award and the Film Critics Circle Award for Best Screenplay. The play won multiple awards including the NSW Premier's Literary Award, the Australian Writers' Guild Award and the Philip Parsons Award. He was the youngest and only dual winner in consecutive years of the NSW Premier's Literary Award, having won for *Strangers in Between* at Griffin Theatre Company in 2005. David Berthold, Tommy's longtime collaborator, directed both these plays. A new UK production of *Strangers in Between* had a return season at The Kings Head last month, whilst *Holding the Man* played across town at Jack Studio also in a new UK production. Tommy's adaptation of Lorca's *Blood Wedding* formed part of the London 2012 Cultural Olympiad. His play *Gwen in Purgatory* (Belvoir/La Boite) won the WA Premier's Award and the prestigious Richard Burton Prize. His other plays include *Troy's House* (Old Fitz/ATYP) and an adaptation of Christopher Marlowe's *Massacre at Paris* (ATYP, directed by David Berthold). He is a graduate of NIDA's directing course. Tommy is currently writing for two miniseries having co-scripted *Devil's Playground* (winner of the 2015 Logie for Most Outstanding Miniseries and AACTA Award for Best Miniseries), as well as developing new works for the stage.

DAVID BERTHOLD Director

David is one of Australia's leading theatre directors. He has directed for most of Australia's major theatres companies, as well as internationally. He is the Artistic Director of Brisbane Festival, one of Australia's largest international arts festivals. He has been Artistic Director of La Boite Theatre Company, Griffin Theatre Company and the Australian Theatre for Young People, Associate Director of Sydney Theatre Company and Artistic Associate of the Queensland Theatre Company. He was the Festival Director of World Interplay 2007, the world's largest festival of young playwrights. He was recently appointed to the Board of Playwriting Australia. David's recent productions include *Hamlet*, *Julius Caesar*, *Ruben Guthrie*, *As You Like It*, *Tender Napalm*, *The Glass Menagerie*, *Cosi*, *I Love You, Bro* (La Boite) and a national tour of the concert drama *Rolling Thunder Vietnam*. He has directed three previous premieres of plays by Tommy Murphy: *Strangers in Between* (Griffin Theatre Company and on tour); the multi-award winning adaptation of Timothy Conigrave's memoir *Holding the Man* (with seasons at Griffin Theatre Company, Sydney Opera House, Belvoir, Melbourne Theatre Company, Brisbane Powerhouse, La Boite and a 2010 season in London's West End); and *Saturn's Return* for Sydney Theatre Company.

Christopher Stollery and Peter Carroll

Helen Thomson

PETER CARROLL Bruce Field / Senior Physician / David / Priest / Iranian Officer

Peter's distinguished career has spanned over 90 productions. He continues to work in music theatre, new Australian texts and the classics. For Belvoir, Peter has appeared in *Twelfth Night or What You Will*, *The Great Fire*, *Seventeen*, *A Christmas Carol*, *Oedipus Rex*, *Old Man*, *The Book of Everything*, *Happy Days*, *Hamlet*, *The Blind Giant is Dancing*, *The Tempest*, *The Chairs* and *Stuff Happens*. His other theatre credits include *Krapp's Last Tape* (State Theatre Company South Australia/MONA FOMO tour); *Last Man Standing* (Melbourne Theatre Company); *Chitty Chitty Bang Bang* (TML Enterprises); *Night on Bald Mountain* (Malthouse Theatre); and *No Man's Land* (Queensland Theatre Company/Sydney Theatre Company). Peter was a member of the Nimrod Theatre Company and the STC Actors Company. Peter has won many awards including Green Room Awards, a Helpmann Award, a Sydney Theatre Critics' Circle Award and an Honorary Doctorate of Creative Arts. Peter is the recipient of the Media Arts & Entertainment Alliance's Lifetime Achievement Award, and he continues to be a proud supporter of the union.

DAMIEN COOPER Lighting Designer

Damien works internationally across theatre, opera and dance. For Belvoir, he has lit *The Great Fire*, *Radiance*, *The Glass Menagerie*, *Coranderrk*, *Miss Julie*, *Stories I Want to Tell You in Person*, *Cat on a Hot Tin Roof*, *Peter Pan*, *Private Lives*, *Conversation Piece*, *Strange Interlude*, *Summer of the Seventeenth Doll*, *Neighbourhood Watch*, *The Seagull*, *Gethsemane*, *Keating!*, *Toy Symphony*, *Peribanez*, *Stuff Happens*, *The Chairs*, *The Spook*, *In Our Name*, *The Underpants*, *The Ham Funeral* and *Exit the King* (including the Broadway production with Geoffrey Rush and Susan Sarandon). His other theatre credits include *Disgraced*, *Orlando*, *Arcadia*, *A Midsummer Night's Dream*, *The Golden Age*, *Suddenly Last Summer*, *The Women of Troy*, *The Lost Echo*, *Riflemind*, *Tot Mom* (Sydney Theatre Company); *Macbeth* and *The Tempest* (Bell Shakespeare). For opera, Damien's designs include *Der Ring des Nibelungen*, *Aida*, *Cosi Fan Tutte* (Opera Australia); *Peter Grimes* (Opera Australia/Canadian Opera Company/Houston Grand Opera); *A Midsummer Night's Dream* (Chicago Lyric Opera/Houston Grand Opera/Canadian Opera Company); *The Magic Flute* (Lyric Opera Chicago); and *Chorus!* (Houston Grand Opera). His designs for dance include *The Narrative of Nothing*, *Firebird*, *Swan Lake* (Australian Ballet); *Am I* (Shaun Parker & Company); *Affinity* (Tasdance); *Mortal Engine* (Chunky Move); and *Of Earth and Sky* (Bangarra Dance Theatre). For lighting design, Damien has won three Sydney Theatre Awards, three Green Room Awards, and two Australian Production Design Guild Awards.

NATE EDMONDSON Composer & Sound Designer

Nate is an international, multi-award winning composer and sound designer for advertising, film, television and stage. For Belvoir, he has been sound designer on *Mortido*, *Seventeen* and *This Heaven*; associate sound designer on *Kill the Messenger*; and assistant sound designer on *Angels in America Parts One & Two*. Nate's other credits include *A Midsummer Night's Dream*, *Romeo and Juliet* (Sydney Theatre Company); *Never Did Me Any Harm* [Associate Sound Designer] (Force Majeure/Sydney Theatre Company); *Once We Were* (Sydney Dance Company); *A Midsummer*

Night's Dream, The Tempest, Romeo And Juliet, As You Like It [Associate Sound Designer], Macbeth, The Winter's Tale (Bell Shakespeare); MinusOneSister, Caress/Ache, The Witches, Music, Jump For Jordan, The Floating World [Assistant Sound Designer], Rust and Bone, This Year's Ashes (Griffin Theatre Company); Salomé, Lord Of The Flies (Malthouse Theatre); Slut, Remembering Pirates, Savages, Daylight Saving, All My Sons, Torch Song Trilogy, The Greening Of Grace, The Seafarer, The Paris Letter (Darlinghurst Theatre); That Golden Girls Show! [US], The Very Hungry Caterpillar Show [US, UK, UAE, NZ, AU] (Rockefeller Productions); Shellshock (Riverside Theatres); Fireface, The Hiding Place (ATYP); Of Mice And Men (Sport For Jove); The Trouble With Harry, Good With Maps, Misterman (Siren Theatre Co.); All My Sons [UK] (Street Theatre); I Hate You My Mother, I Am My Own Wife, A Girl With Sun In Her Eyes, Freak Winds (Red Line Productions); Marat/Sade, When The Rain Stops Falling, Julius Caesar (New Theatre); Two By Two, Suddenly Last Summer (Little Ones Theatre); Leaves and Straight (KXT).

KIT ESURUOSO William Colvin / Junior Physician / Martin / BBC Radio Journalist / Tom / Charon / Kane

Kit graduated from Mountview Academy in London in 2015. His theatre credits include Show Boat (West End and Sheffield Crucible) and The Last Days of Troy (Shakespeare's Globe). Kit has also been a soloist in A Night Full Of Song and Mountview's 70th Anniversary Concert, and a vocalist for Elaine Paige at Royal Albert Hall. His television credits include Autopsy (ITV) and he is the lead in the upcoming feature film Akoni. He has also worked in radio and advertising, and performed in many productions at Mountview Academy. Mark Colvin's Kidney marks Kit's debut at Belvoir.

MICHAEL HANKIN Set Designer

Michael is a NIDA trained set and costume designer for theatre and film. His credits for Belvoir include Jasper Jones, Twelfth Night or What You Will, The Great Fire, Ivanov, A Christmas Carol, The Glass Menagerie, Angels in America and The Dark Room. Michael's other theatre credits include Jumpy (Melbourne Theatre Company/Sydney Theatre Company); Lake Disappointment (Carriageworks); Othello, As You Like It (Bell Shakespeare); The Aspirations of Daise Morrow (Brink Productions, Adelaide); Ich Nibber Dibber (Sydney Festival/Campbelltown Arts Centre); Dirty Rotten Scoundrels (Theatre Royal); Of Mice and Men (Sport for Jove); 247 Days (Chunky Move/Malthouse Theatre/Netherlands tour); Tartuffe (State Theatre Company South Australia); Ugly Mugs (Malthouse Theatre/Griffin Theatre Company); Truckstop (Q Theatre/Seymour Centre); Songs for the Fallen (Sydney Festival/New York Music Theatre Festival); The Peasant Prince (Monkey Baa); Rust and Bone, The Ugly One (Griffin Theatre Company); Obscura (Force Majeure/Carriageworks); Fool for Love (Company B/Savage Productions); Miracle City (Hayes Theatre); The Boat People (TRS/The Hayloft Project); The Lighthouse, In The Penal Colony (Sydney Chamber Opera); Liberty Equality Fraternity, Great Falls (Ensemble Theatre); Deathtrap, Miss Julie, The Paris Letter, Macbeth (Darlinghurst Theatre); Suddenly Last Summer and Women of Troy (The Cell Block Theatre). His short films include Julian and The Amber Amulet (both winners of the Crystal Bear, Berlin International Film Festival). Michael has received Sydney Theatre Awards for Best Independent Stage Design for Of Mice and Men in 2015 and Truckstop in 2012, as well as numerous nominations. Michael is currently Associate Lecturer of Design at NIDA.

JOHN HOWARD Mark Colvin

John graduated from NIDA in 1978 and his career has seen him work on the stage, in cinema and television. For Belvoir, he has appeared in *Twelfth Night or What You Will*, *Ivanov*, *Every Breath* and *A Doll's House*. His other theatre work includes *All My Sons*, *The Crucible*, *Dead White Males*, *The Life of Galileo*, *Mongrels*, *The Recruit* (Sydney Theatre Company); *Shrine*, *Rising Water* (Black Swan State Theatre Company); and *The Rover* (State Theatre Company South Australia). John was appointed Associate Director of the Sydney Theatre Company in 1992. His film roles include *Mad Max: Fury Road*, *Last Cab to Darwin*, *The Man Who Sued God*, *A Man's Gotta Do* and *Jindabyne*. In TV, John has appeared in many diverse shows including *Soul Mates*, *Janet King*, *SeaChange*, *All Saints*, *Always Greener*, *Packed to the Rafters* and the miniseries *Changi*. John's awards include a 2015 Sydney Theatre Award for Best Supporting Actor in a Mainstage Production for *Ivanov* and a Sydney Critics' Circle Award for Best Stage Actor in 1991. He won his first Silver Logie for Most Outstanding Actor for his role in *SeaChange* in 2001.

JULIE LYNCH Costume Designer

Julie has worked extensively as a designer for drama, television, opera, dance and exhibition. Her most recent theatre credits include designing *The Tempest* for Bell Shakespeare and *Arms and the Man* and *Arcadia* for Sydney Theatre Company. Julie has won four Sydney Theatre Awards, two Helpmann Awards, two APDG Awards and one Green Room Award for Costume Design. Julie also has experience designing for large scale events including costume design for Opera Australia's Handa Opera production of *Carmen* on Sydney Harbour, and *Stations of the Cross* for World Youth Day, performed on and around Sydney Harbour and broadcast around the world. Julie has wide-ranging experience as an educator and administrator. She is MFA Design lecturer at NIDA and was Head of Costume there from 2000 to 2005. She has been a member of NIDA's Academic Board, a Board Member of the NIDA Company, and is Vice President of the Australian Production Design Guild (APDG). In 2013, Julie attained a Master of Arts by Research degree, and is currently completing her Doctorate at the University of Sydney – Department of Performance Studies.

Sarah Peirse

Kit Esuruoso and John Howard

LUKE McGETTIGAN Stage Manager

Luke is Belvoir's Resident Stage Manager. For Belvoir, he has stage managed *Faith Healer*, *Twelfth Night or What You Will*, *The Great Fire*, *Mortido*, *Seventeen*, *Elektra/Orestes*, *Radiance*, *The Glass Menagerie*, *Brothers Wreck*, *Once in Royal David's City*, *Miss Julie*, *Forget Me Not*, *Peter Pan* (including New York tour), *Private Lives*, *Death of a Salesman*, *Babyteeth*, *Summer of the Seventeenth Doll*, *Neighbourhood Watch*, *The Wild Duck* (including UK and Europe tours), *Namatjira* (Belvoir/Big hART), *Page 8*, *The End*, *That Face*, *The Promise*, *Scorched*, *Antigone*, *Keating!*, *The Little Cherry Orchard* and *The Caucasian Chalk Circle*. His other credits include *The Pig Iron People*, *The Give and Take*, *Bed*, *La Dispute* (Sydney Theatre Company); *Like a Fishbone* (Sydney Theatre Company/ Griffin Theatre Company); *The Government Inspector*, *The Tempest*, *The Servant of Two Masters*, *The Comedy of Errors*, *The Taming of the Shrew* (Bell Shakespeare); *Paradise City*, *Through the Wire* (Performing Lines); *Alive at Williamstown Pier* (Griffin Theatre Company); *Scam*, *Abroad With Two Men* (Christine Dunstan Productions); *Flexitime*, *Market Forces*, *Shoe Horn Sonata*, *Blinded by the Sun* (Ensemble Theatre); *The Complete Works of William Shakespeare* (Spirit Productions); *Twelfth Night*, *Arms and the Man*, *Much Ado About Nothing*, *Spring Awakening* (Railway Street Theatre Company); *Barmaids*, *Radiance* (New England Theatre Company); *My Girragundji* (Canute Productions); and *Dog Logs* (Marguerite Pepper Productions).

SARAH PEIRSE Mary-Ellen Field

Sarah is one of Australia and New Zealand's most respected and awarded actresses. For Belvoir, she has performed in *The Business* and *Gethsemane*. Her other recent stage credits include *The Golden Age*, *Endgame*, *Switzerland*, *Poor Boy*, *Fury*, *Dead Funny* (Sydney Theatre Company); *Switzerland*, *Tribes*, *Poor Boy*, *Enlightenment*, *Molly Sweeney*, *The Heidi Chronicles* (Melbourne Theatre Company); *Other Desert Cities* and *The Gift* (Auckland Theatre Company). Sarah has won a Helpmann Award for Best Female Actor in a Supporting Role for *The Golden Age*, a Sydney Theatre Award for Best Lead Actress in *Switzerland* and a Green Room Award for Best Performance by a Female Actress for *Molly Sweeney*. Sarah will next be seen in the ABC miniseries *Seven Types Of Ambiguity* and most recently appeared in Network Ten's *Offspring*, the US series *Hunters* for SyFy and the ABC comedy pilot *The Let Down*. Her other television credits include *The Shannara Chronicles*, *Old School*, *Rake*, *Bliss: A Story Of Katherine Mansfield*, *City Homicide*, *Spirited*, *Murder Rooms*, *Water Rats*, *Fable* and *The Flying Doctors*. Her film credits include award-winning performances in *Heavenly Creatures*, *Rain* and *The Navigator*. She also featured in two films in *The Hobbit Trilogy*, *The Hopes & Dreams Of Gazza Snell*, *Unconditional Love*, *The Illustrated Family Doctor* and *The Art Of Drowning*.

KEIREN SMITH Assistant Stage Manager

For Belvoir, **Keiren** has been stage manager on *La Traviata* and assistant stage manager on *The Drover's Wife*, *Back at the Dojo*, *Mother Courage and Her Children*, *Radiance*, *Nora*, *Brothers Wreck* and *Once in Royal David's City*. She has an Advanced Diploma in Stage Management from WAAPA and a Bachelor of Arts in Communication and Cultural Studies from Curtin University. Keiren was assistant stage manager with The Australian Ballet for three years, touring domestically and internationally including to Japan and New York, working on many repertoire and new ballets such as *Don Quixote*, *Onegin*, *The Merry Widow*, *Madame Butterfly*, *Coppelia*, *The Nutcracker*, *The Silver Rose*, Alexei Ratmansky's *Cinderella*, Stephen Bayne's *Swan Lake* and Graeme Murphy's *Romeo and Juliet*. Her other credits as assistant stage manager include *Theodora* (Pinchgut Opera); *Hay Fever* (Sydney Theatre Company); *Solomon and Marion* (Melbourne Theatre Company); *The Web*, *Much Ado About Nothing* (Black Swan State Theatre Company); and Sydney New Year's Eve – Lord Mayor's Party (City of Sydney).

CHRISTOPHER STOLLERY Professor Zoltan Endre / John Colvin / Carl / Lucas / BBC Radio Studio Guest / Emad

Christopher is a graduate of NIDA. He has sung with Tim Minchin in the musical *This Blasted Earth* (2004), performed with John Cleese at the Sydney Opera House (*Just For Laughs*, 2012), and toured theatres of Europe with Cate Blanchett (*Gross und Klein* for Sydney Theatre Company, 2012). Christopher was also an associate artist with Bell Shakespeare Company, appearing in 19 productions. His other theatre credits include *Death of a Salesman*, *The Power of Yes*, *Ruben Guthrie*, *Killer Joe* (Belvoir); *Rosencrantz & Guildenstern Are Dead*, *Our Town*, *The Vertical Hour* (Sydney Theatre Company); *His Girl Friday* (Melbourne Theatre Company); *Good People*, *Great Falls* (Ensemble Theatre); *Daylight Saving* (Darlinghurst Theatre); *Speaking in Tongues*, *October* (Griffin Theatre Company); *Julius Caesar/Antony and Cleopatra* and *Of Mice and Men* (Sport for Jove). He has been nominated for a Green Room Award twice and won a Sydney Theatre Award in 2009 for his performance of the title role in *Killer Joe* (Belvoir). He has also appeared as a regular character on many television series including *Wild Boys*, *Sea Patrol*, *State Corner* and *The Flying Doctors*. His film credits include *Last Cab to Darwin*, *Predestination* and *The Rage in Placid Lake*. Christopher is also a graduate of AFTRS and his short films have won over 30 awards internationally. Christopher is a proud member of Equity since 1987.

HELEN THOMSON Elle Macpherson / Michele / Cassandra / BBC Radio Journalist / Nurse Sunita / French Parishioner / American Operator / Waitress

For Belvoir, **Helen** has appeared in *Ivanov*, *Summer of the Seventeenth Doll* and *Measure for Measure*. She will also appear in *Hir* for Belvoir in 2017. Helen's other theatre credits include *After Dinner*, *Children of the Sun*, *Mrs Warren's Profession*, *In The Next Room (or The Vibrator Play)*, *The Splinter*, *God of Carnage*, *A Midsummer Night's Dream*, *Art Of War*, *The Season at Sarsaparilla*, *Macbeth*, *The Virgin Mim*, *School for Scandal*, *The John Wayne Principle*, *The Shaughraun*, *Arcadia* (Sydney Theatre Company); *Hinterland*, *Much Ado About Nothing*, *The Dutch Courtesan*, *A View from the Bridge*, *Othello*, *The Selection* (Melbourne Theatre Company); *The Winter's Tale*, *Troilus and Cressida* (Bell Shakespeare Company); *Cruise Control* (Ensemble Theatre); *Footprints on Water* (Neonheart Theatre Company); *Chilling and Killing My Annabel Lee*, *Coralie Lansdowne Says No* (Griffin Theatre Company); and *The Crucible* (Queensland Theatre Company). On film, Helen has appeared in *A Man's Gotta Do*, *Gettin' Square*, *Kangaroo Jack*, *La Spagnola*, *Strange Planet* and *Thank God He Met Lizzie*. Her television credits include *Doctor Doctor*, *Love Child*, *Rake*, *Catching Milat*, *Wonderland*, *Mr and Mrs Murder*, *Bastard Boys*, *Stupid Stupid Man*, *Blackjack*, *Blue Heelers*, *Bad Cop* and the web series *Avalon Now*. Helen won a Helpmann Award in 2015 for *After Dinner* (Sydney Theatre Company) and has received numerous nominations.

VEXRAN PRODUCTIONS Projection Design

Vexran Productions is a boutique agency that designs visual content and provides technical design for live theatre and events. It brings together the talents of an experienced lighting designer in Verity Hampson and film and TV producer Xanon Murphy. Vexran Productions has previously worked on *The Blind Giant is Dancing* (Belvoir); *The Turquoise Elephant*, *Beached* [co-design with Steve Toulmin] (Griffin Theatre Company); *Before/After* (Sydney Theatre Company); *Crown Prince Couple's Awards* (Sydney Opera House/SBS/Danish Broadcasting Corporation); *In the Penal Colony* (Sydney Chamber Opera); *Great Falls* (Ensemble Theatre); *Small Things* (B Sharp); and *Parramatta Girls* (Riverside Theatres). Xanon's other credits include producer on *The Roast* (ABC TV), *The Last Trimate* (Animal Planet), the feature documentaries *Decadence: Decline of the Western World* and *Blood On The Coal*, as well as numerous corporate videos for major brands and clients.

SCOTT WITT Movement Director

Scott is an award-winning artist who has worked for 30 years as a writer/adaptor, fight director, movement consultant, actor, director and clown. As a fight director and/or movement consultant, his theatre credits number well over 250 professional productions including *Jasper Jones*, *The Drover's Wife*, *Back at the Dojo*, *The Events*, *Mortido*, *Ivanov*, *Seventeen*, *Mother Courage and Her Children*, *Samson*, *Elektra/Orestes*, *Kill the Messenger*, *Radiance*, *A Christmas Carol*, *Hedda Gabler*, *Oedipus Schmoedipus*, *Miss Julie*, *Angels in America*, *Peter Pan*, *Beautiful One Day*, *Medea*, *Private Lives*, *Death of a Salesman*, *Babyteeth*, *The Dark Room*, *Summer of the Seventeenth Doll*, *Gwen in Purgatory*, *That Face* (Belvoir); *All My Sons*, *Disgraced*, *King Lear*, *Suddenly Last Summer*, *After Dinner*, *Noises Off*, *Waiting for Godot*, *Rosencrantz and Guildenstern Are Dead*, *The Fury*, *The Secret River*, *Mariage Blanc*, *Signs of Life*, *Les Liaisons Dangereuses*, *Zebra*, *God of Carnage*, *True West*, *A Streetcar Named Desire*, *The Wonderful World of Dissocia* (Sydney Theatre Company); *Fawlty Towers* (McIntyre & Coppel); *The Tempest*, *As You Like It*, *Tartuffe*, *Henry V*, *Comedy of Errors*, *Henry IV*, *The Taming of the Shrew* (Bell Shakespeare); *Monkey* (Theatre of Image); *Death and the Maiden*, *Private Lives* (Melbourne Theatre Company); *Taming of the Shrew*, *Edward II*, *Cyrano*, *Othello*, *Comedy of Errors*, *Hamlet* (Sport for Jove); *The Pearlfishers*, *Rabbits*, *Faust*, *Rigoletto*, *Macbeth*, *Don Giovanni* (Opera Australia); *Anatomy Titus: Fall of Rome*, *The Alchemist*, *Richard III* (Bell Shakespeare/Queensland Theatre Company); *Macbeth*, *Toy Symphony*, *The Crucible*, *School of Arts*, *Stones in His Pockets*, *Who's Afraid of Virginia Woolf?*, *The Glass Menagerie* and *Private Lives* (Queensland Theatre Company). Scott has been a proud platinum member of MEAA since 1988, and is the current Artistic Director of the International Order of the Sword & the Pen.

ORGAN DONATION

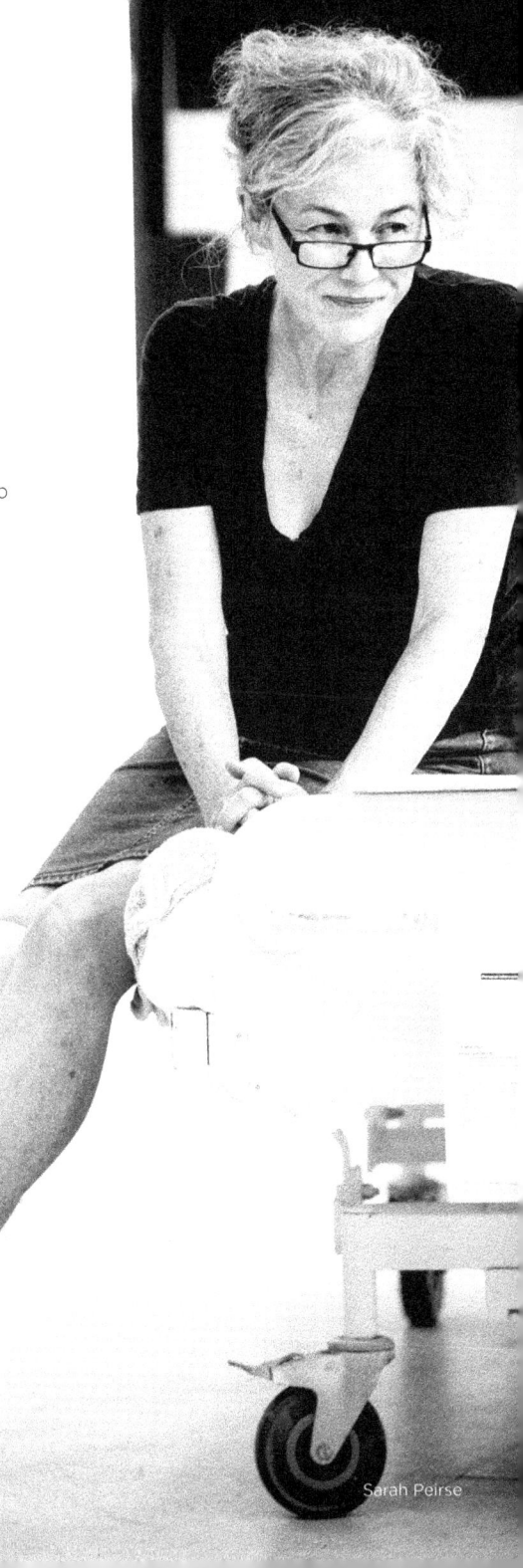

Organ donation saves lives as this play illustrates. Australia has one of the best survival rates for all organ transplants but we fall behind in donations. Most donations come from deceased donors. Kidneys and sometimes part of the liver can also be donated by living donors who are close relatives or friends.

Although registering as a donor through the national organ donor registry provides the donor medical team with your intention, they *always* contact your family for confirmation as you may have changed your mind. It is essential that you make your intention known to your next of kin to ensure they can comfortably confirm your decision to donate your organs after you die. It is very important to have this family conversation so you can be certain that your wishes are respected.

For more information about organ donation in Australia and how to join the national organ donor registry, visit **www.donatelife.gov.au**.

Donations for kidney and transplant research at the Prince of Wales Hospital can be made at **www.powhf.org.au**.

Professor Zoltán H. Endre
Head, Department of Nephrology, Prince of Wales Hospital, Sydney

Sarah Peirse

BELVOIR

THEATRICALITY.
VARIETY OF LIFE.
FAITH IN HUMANITY.

Belvoir is a theatre company on a side street in Surry Hills, Sydney. We share our street with a park and a public housing estate, and our theatre is in an old industrial building. It has been, at various times, a garage, a sauce factory, and the Nimrod Theatre. When the theatre was threatened with redevelopment in 1984, more than 600 people formed a syndicate to buy the building and save the theatre. Thirty years later, Belvoir St Theatre continues to be home to one of Australia's most celebrated theatre companies.

In its early years Belvoir was run cooperatively. It later rose to international prominence under first and longest-serving Artistic Director Neil Armfield and continued to be both wildly successful and controversial under Ralph Myers. Belvoir is a traditional home for the great old crafts of acting and story in Australian theatre. It is a platform for voices that won't otherwise be heard. And it is a gathering of outspoken ideals. In short: theatricality, variety of life, and faith in humanity.

At Belvoir we gather the best theatre artists we can find, emerging and established, to realise an annual season of works – new Australian plays, Indigenous works, re-imagined classics and new international writing. Audiences remember many landmark productions including *The Drover's Wife*, *Angels in America*, *Brothers Wreck*, *The Glass Menagerie*, *Neighbourhood Watch*, *The Wild Duck*, *Medea*, *The Diary of a Madman*, *Death of a Salesman*, *The Blind Giant is Dancing*, *Hamlet*, *Cloudstreet*, *Aliwa*, *The Book of Everything*, *Keating!*, *The Exile Trilogy*, *Exit the King*, *The Sapphires* and *Who's Afraid of Virginia Woolf?*

Today, under Artistic Director Eamon Flack and Executive Director Brenna Hobson, Belvoir tours nationally and internationally, and continues to create its own brand of rough magic for new generations of audiences.

Belvoir receives government support for its activities from the federal government through the Major Performing Arts Panel of the Australia Council and the state government through Arts NSW. We also welcome and warmly appreciate all philanthropic support.

belvoir.com.au

BELVOIR STAFF

18 Belvoir Street, Surry Hills NSW 2010
Email mail@belvoir.com.au Web belvoir.com.au
Administration (02) 9698 3344 Facsimile (02) 9319 3165 Box Office (02) 9699 3444

Artistic Director
Eamon Flack
Executive Director
Brenna Hobson
Deputy Executive Director & Head of Development
Aaron Beach

BELVOIR BOARD
Anne Britton
Mitchell Butel
Luke Carroll
Tracey Driver
Eamon Flack
Brenna Hobson
Ian Learmonth
Samantha Meers (Chair)
Peter Wilson

BELVOIR ST THEATRE BOARD
Stuart McCreery
Angela Pearman (Chair)
Sue Rosen
Nick Schlieper
Mark Seymour
Kingsley Slipper
Susan Teasey

ARTISTIC & PROGRAMMING
Associate Director – New Work
Anthea Williams
Associate Artist
Tom Wright
Artistic Associate
Nell Ranney

EDUCATION
Education Manager
Jane May
Education Coordinator
Simone Evans

ADMINISTRATION
Artistic Administrator
John Woodland

FINANCE & OPERATIONS
Company Accountant
Komal Rabadiya
Accounts Administrator
Susan Jack
IT & Operations Manager
Jan S. Goldfeder

BOX OFFICE & CUSTOMER SERVICES
Customer Experience & Ticketing Manager
Andrew Dillon
Ticketing Systems Administrator
Tanya Ginori-Cairns
CRM Manager
Charlotte Bradley

FRONT OF HOUSE
Front of House Manager
Ohmeed Ahi
Assistant Front of House Manager
Scott Pirlo

DEVELOPMENT
Philanthropy Managers
Joanna Maunder & Liz Tomkinson
Development Coordinator
Jessica Vincent

MARKETING
Head of Marketing & Customer Service
Amy Goodhew
Marketing Coordinator
Georgia Goode
Communications Coordinator
Cara Nash
Publicity & Public Affairs Manager
Elly Baxter

PRODUCTION
Head of Production
Sally Withnell
Production Coordinator
Eliza Maunsell
Technical Manager
Will Jacobs
Resident Stage Manager
Luke McGettigan
Staging & Construction Manager
Penny Angrick
Staging & Construction Assistant
Brydie Ryan
Costume Coordinator
Judy Tanner
Senior Technician
Caitlin Porter
Commercial Construction Manager
Simon Boyd

BELVOIR DONORS

We give our heartfelt thanks to all our donors for their loyal and generous support.

CREATIVE DEVELOPMENT FUND

$10,000+
Andrew Cameron AM
& Cathy Cameron**
Helen Lynch AM & Helen Bauer**
Frank Macindoe*
Samantha Meers
Sherry-Hogan Foundation*
Kim Williams AM & Catherine Dovey

$5,000 - $9,999
Anonymous (1)
Stephen Allen
Anne Britton**
Hartley Cook*
Gail Hambly*
Louise Herron AM & Clark Butler**
Peter & Rosemary Ingle*
Don & Leslie Parsonage
Dan & Jackie Phillips
Doc Ross Family Foundation
Victoria Taylor**
Shemara Wikramanayake
& Ed Gilmartin

$2,000 - $4,999
Neil Armfield AO**
Jill & Richard Berry
Justin Butterworth & Stephen Asher
John Cary
Janet & Trefor Clayton*
Michael Coleman*
Bob & Chris Ernst
Lisa Hamilton & Rob White
Victoria Holthouse*
David Robb

$500 - $1,999
Helen Argiris
Richard Banks
Tim Bishop
Chris Collett
Joanna Collins
Michael Dowe
Linda English
Phillip English
Timothy Hale
Roey Higgs
Michael Hobbs
Stephanie Hutchinson
Angus Hutchinson
Alec Leopold
Janine Perrett*
Steve Rankine
Richard, Heather & Rachel Rasker
Penelope Seidler
Alenka Tindale
Mark Warburton
Penny Ward
Sheryl Weil

CO-CONSPIRATORS

$10,000+
Gail Hambly**
Anita Jacoby*
David Pumphrey
Mark Warburton
Cathy Yuncken

THE CHAIR'S GROUP

$3,000+
Judge Joe Harman
Marion Heathcote & Brian Burfitt**

$1,000 - $2,999
Antoinette Albert**
Jill & Richard Berry
Jillian Broadbent AO**
Chris Brown
Jan Chapman AO &
Stephen O'Rourke**
Wesley Enoch
Kathleen & Danny Gilbert**
Sophie Guest
Michael Hobbs*
Hilary Linstead**
Ross McLean & Fiona Beith*
Cajetan Mula (Honorary Member)
Sherry-Hogan Foundation
Steve Rankine
Alex Oonagh Redmond**
Michael Rose
Ann Sherry AO*
Penny Ward*
David & Jennifer Watson**
Kim Williams AM**

B KEEPERS

$5,000+
Robert & Libby Albert**
Ellen Borda*
Constructability Recruitment
Marion Heathcote & Brian Burfitt**
Bruce Meagher & Greg Waters
Don & Leslie Parsonage*

$3,000 - $4,999
Anonymous (1)
Bev & Phil Birnbaum**
Anne Britton**
Louise Christie**
Tom Dent
Suzanne & Michael Daniel**
Bob & Chris Ernst**
Robyn Godlee & Tony Maxwell
David & Kathryn Groves*
Colleen Kane**
S Khouri & D Cross
Chantal & Greg Roger **
Peter & Jan Shuttleworth*
Jann Skinner
Merilyn Sleigh & Raoul de Ferranti

$2,000 - $2,999
Claire Armstrong & John Sharpe**
Dr. Kimberly Cartwright &
Mr. Charles Littrell
Cary & Rob Gillespie
Peter Graves**
David Haertsch**
John Head**
Jennifer Ledgar & Bob Lim*
Louise Mitchell & Peter Pether
Dr David Nguyen*
Timothy & Eva Pascoe**
Lesley & Andrew Rosenberg*
Judy Thomson*
Lynne Watkins & Nicholas Harding*

$1,000 - $1,999
Anonymous (2)
Berg Family Foundation**
Max Bonnell**
Charlene & Graham Bradley AM
Dr Catherine Brown-Watt PSM
Jan Burnswoods*
Mary Jo & Lloyd Capps**
Elaine Chia
Jane Christensen*
Jeanne Eve**
Lisa Hamilton & Rob White
Wendy & Andrew Hamlin**
Libby Higgin*
Michael Hobbs**
Susan Ingram
Avril Jeans**
Kevin & Rosemarie Jeffers-Palmer **
Corinne & Rob Johnston*
Margaret Johnston
A. le Marchant*
Professor Elizabeth More AM**
Stephanie Lee*
Atul Lele*
Hilary Linstead**
Christopher Matthies
K Nomchong SC
Jacqueline & Michael Palmer
Dr Natalie Pelham*
Greeba Pritchard*
David & Jill Pumphrey
Richard, Heather & Rachel Rasker*
Richmond Sisters
Colleen Roche
David Round
Andrew & Louise Sharpe*
Jennifer Smith
Chris & Bea Sochan*
Jeremy Storer & Annabel Crabb
Camilla & Andrew Strang
Sue Thomson*
Alese Watson
Paul & Jennifer Winch

THE HIVE

$2,500
Anthony & Elly Baxter
Nathan & Yael Bennett
Justin Butterworth & Stephen Asher
Dan & Emma Chesterman
Este Darin-Cooper & Chris Burgess
Joanna Davidson & Julian Leeser
Tracey Driver
Jeremy Goff & Amelia Morgan-Hunn
Piers Grove
Ruth Higgins & Tamson Pietsch
Emma Hogan & Kim Hogan
G W Outram & F E Holyoake
David Rayment & Mary Nguyen
Andrew & Louise Sharpe*
Michael Sirmai & Rebecca Finkelstein
Chris Smith
Saurabh Thaper
The Sky Foundation
Jourdan Thompson

HONEY Bs

$1,000+
Margaret Butler
Marla Heller
Tristan Landers
Louise McCoach
Samantha Meers
Olivia Pascoe
Janet Pennington
Sylvia Preda
Janna Robertson
Arlene Tansey
Lauren Thompson
Cathy Yuncken

EDUCATION DONORS

$10,000+
Doc Ross Family Foundation
Margaret Butler
Susie & Nick Kelly
Ian Learmonth & Julia Pincus

$2,000 - $4,999
Anonymous (3)
Ian Barnett*
Andrew Cameron AM &
Cathy Cameron**
Estate of the late Angelo Comino
Ari Droga
Julie Hannaford*
Judge Joe Harman
Bill Hawker
Olivia Pascoe**

$500 - $1,999
32 Edward St
Anonymous (4)
Len & Nita Armfield
AB*
Arrow Commodities
Art House Gallery
David Bennett AO & Anne Bennett
Judy Binns
Michael & Colleen Chesterman*
Esther Helen Cossman
Tracey Clancy
Karen Cooper & Simon Tuxen
Erin Devery
Diane Dunlop*
Denise & Robert Dunn
Veronica Espaliat &
Ross Youngman
John B Fairfax AO & Libby Fairfax
Laurie Foal
Suzy Gellert
Geoffrey & Patricia Gemmell*
Peter Gray
Bill Hawker
Dorothy Hoddinott AO**
Sue Hyde*
Peter & Rosemary Ingle*
David Jonas & Desmon Du Plessis

Catherine Jones
Stewart & Jillian Kellie*
Xanthi Kouvatas
Veronica & Matthew Latham
Ruth Layton
Jennifer Ledgar & Bob Lim*
Damian Lovell
Annabelle Mahar
David Marr & Sebastian Tesoriero
Pamela Mcgaw
Mary Miltenyi
Patricia Novikoff
Plaza Films
Polese Family
Nigel Poole
Richard, Heather & Rachel Rasker
Angela Raymond
Ruth Ritchie
Geoffrey Rush AC
Peter & Janet Shuttleworth*
Nawal Silfani
Chris & Bea Sochan*
Kerry Stubbs
Drew Tait
Daniela Torsh
Ingrid Villata
Richard & Sue Walsh
Andrew Watts
Ali Yeldham

GENERAL DONORS

$10,000+
Anonymous (1)
Andrew Cameron AM
& Cathy Cameron**
Ross Littlewood
& Alexandra Curtin*

$2,000 - $4,999
Anonymous (2)
Richard Evans
Brenna Hobson
Anita Jacoby*
Raymond McDonald
Ralph Myers
Patricia Novikoff*
Lynne Watkins & Nicolas Harding*

$500 - $1,999
Anonymous (5)
Victor Baskir
Baiba Berzins*
Christine Bishop
Allen & Julie Blewitt
Mr Dennis Bluth & Dr Diana Marks
Keith Bradley AM
Ian Breden & Josephine Key*
Anne Britton**
Angela Bowne
Trevor Carroll
Colleen & Michael Chesterman
Esther Helen Cossman
Tim & Bryony Cox*

Jane Diamond*
Elizabeth Fairfax
Gillian Fenton
Sandra Ferman
Jono Gavin
Tim Gerrard
Peter Gray & Helen Thwaites
Priscilla Guest*
Dr Cheryl Hanbury
Kim Harding & Irene Miller
Harrison & Kate Higgs*
Dorothy Hoddinott AO**
Clyth Hoult
Robert Kidd
Daniel Knight
Wolf Krueger & José Gutierrez*
Franz Lauenstein
Lisa Manchur
Wailyn Mar
Julianne Maxwell
E.J.R McDonald
Julian Meagher
Irene Miller
Dr David and Barbara Millons
Irena Nebenzahl
Louise & Michael Nettleton
Patricia Novikoff*
Anthony Nugent
Judy & Geoff Patterson*
Dr Natalie Pelham
Georgina Perry
Kathirasen Ponnusamy*
Kim Rosser
Leigh Sanderson
Elfriede Sangkuhl
Abhijit & Janice Sengupta
Dr Agnes Sinclair
Eileen Slarke & Family**
Alexia Smyth-Kirk
Andrea Socratous
Dr Titia Sprague
Paul Stein
Yael Stone
Axel & Diane Tennie
Mike Thompson
Gayle Tollifson
Helen Trinca
Suzanne & Ross Tzannes AM*
Jane Uebergang
Louise & Steve Verrier
Chris Vik & Chelsea Albert
Sarah Walters*
Mark Warburton
Louisa Ward & Tim Coen
Dr Rosemary White
Brian & Trish Wright

* 5+ years of giving
** 10+ years of giving
*** 15+ years of giving

List correct at time of printing.

Belvoir is very grateful to accept donations of all sizes. Donations over $2 are tax deductible. If you would like to make a donation or would like further information about any of our donor programs please call our Development Team on 02 9698 3344 or email development@belvoir.com.au

BELVOIR DONORS *Continued*

SPECIAL THANKS

We would like to acknowledge Cajetan Mula, Len Armfield and Geoffrey Scharer. They will always be remembered for their generosity to Belvoir.

We also thank our Life Members, who have made outstanding contributions to Belvoir over more than thirty years. They have changed the course of the company and are now ingrained in its fabric: Neil Armfield AO, Neil Balnaves AO, Andrew Cameron AM, David Gonski AC, Rachel Healy, Louise Herron AM, Sue Hill, Geoffrey Rush AC, Orli Wargon OAM and Chris Westwood.

These people and foundations supported the redevelopment of Belvoir St Theatre and purchase of our warehouse.

Andrew & Cathy Cameron
(refurbishment of theatre & warehouse)

Russell Crowe
(Downstairs theatre &
purchase of warehouse)

The Gonski Foundation
& Nelson Meers Foundation
(Gonski Meers Foyer)

Andrew & Wendy Hamlin
(Brenna's office)

Hal Herron
(The Hal Bar)

Geoffrey Rush
(redevelopment of theatre)

Fred Street AM
(Upstairs dressing room)

Baker McKenzie.

Proudly supporting
Belvoir since 1994

www.bakermckenzie.com/australia

How can our performance help yours?

EY's support of the arts helps institutions to grow, innovate and become more accessible to our local communities.

ey.com/au/arts

The better the question.
The better the answer.
The better the world works.

© 2015 Ernst & Young, Australia. All Rights Reserved. Liability limited by a scheme approved under Professional Standards Legislation. S1629338. EDNone. APAC No. AU00002474

EY
Building a better working world

BELVOIR ARTISTS
CHOOSE TO STAY AT

BOUTIQUE HOTEL · STUDIO APARTMENTS
REGENTS COURT
– EST. 1990 –

T +61 2 9331 2099

info@regentscourtsydney.com.au
www.regentscourtsydney.com.au

18 Springfield Avenue
Potts Point NSW 2011

BELVOIR'S ACCOMMODATION SPONSOR

BELVOIR SPONSORS

MAJOR SPONSORS

Baker McKenzie.

MEDIA PARTNERS

IT PARTNER

ASSOCIATE SPONSORS

KEY SUPPORTER

 Indigenous theatre at Belvoir supported by The Balnaves Foundation

EVENT SPONSORS

   the devonshire

GOVERNMENT PARTNERS

YOUTH & EDUCATION SUPPORTER

TRUSTS & FOUNDATIONS

Coca-Cola Australia Foundation
Gandevia Foundation
The Greatorex Foundation
Nelson Meers Foundation
Thyne Reid Foundation

SUPPORTERS

Macquarie Group
Thomas Creative
Time Out Australia

PRODUCTION SPONSORS

For more information on partnership opportunities please contact our Development team on 02 9698 3344 or email development@belvoir.com.au

Correct at time of printing.

ALSO BY TOMMY MURPHY
AND AVAILABLE FROM CURRENCY PRESS

Gwen in Purgatory
Gwen is 90. She woke up this morning to discover that purgatory is sitting alone in a new house in a new subdivision on the edge of town, trying to work out if the remote in her hand operates the TV, the air-con or the fanforced oven. But the kids are coming round and Father Ezekiel is on his way to bless the house, so the beginning of the end is looking up... Written specially for Company B, Gwen in Purgatory is Tommy Murphy's brilliant existential comedy about an African missionary in the wilderness of Australian suburbia. Gwen's brood of ordinary souls is battling along in a changing world and wringing out the last drops of their matriarch's faith. Between them they may just find their way to some sort of forgiveness. Winner of the 2010 WA Premier's Award.
ISBN 9780868198941

Holding the Man and Strangers in Between
Timothy Conigrave's celebrated memoir *Holding the Man* won the 1995 UN Human Rights Award for Non-Fiction and was voted one of Australia's top 100 most favourite books. Tommy Murphy's stage adaptation faithfully captures the book's heart-wrenchingly honest portrayal of a fifteen-year relationship, but also succeeds in transforming it into a unique theatrical experience that is wholly his own. Winner of the 2007 NSW Premier's Literary Award - Play Award.

Strangers in Between is Shane's story. He has fled his family and is seeking refuge in Sydney's Kings Cross. Confused and naïve, he meets two strangers: the ultra-urban Will, who offers brotherhood, sex and something unexpected; and Peter, a fifty-year-old gay man whose mother is dying in a nursing home. With their help – or hindrance – Shane grapples to reconcile himself with events from his past. But how can he move on when he can't even use laundry powder? Winner of the 2006 NSW Premier's Literary Award - Play Award.
ISBN 9780868197968

www.currency.com.au

Visit Currency Press' website now to:

- Buy your books online
- Browse through our full list of titles, from plays to screenplays, books on theatre, film and music, and more
- Choose a play for your school or amateur performance group by cast size and gender
- Obtain information about performance rights
- Find out about theatre productions and other performing arts news across Australia
- For students, read our study guides
- For teachers, access syllabus and other relevant information
- Sign up for our email newsletter

The performing arts publisher

www.ingramcontent.com/pod-product-compliance
Lightning Source LLC
Chambersburg PA
CBHW050017090426
42734CB00021B/3300